THE ORNAMENTED CHAIR

Its Development in America

(1700—1890)

THE ORNAMENTED CHAIR

Its Development in America

(1700—1890)

Edited by ZILLA RIDER LEA

Publication of the Esther Stevens Brazer Guild
of the
Historical Society of Early American Decoration, Inc.

CHARLES E. TUTTLE COMPANY
RUTLAND, VERMONT

Representatives

For Continental Europe:
BOXERBOOKS, INC., *Zurich*

For the British Isles:
PRENTICE-HALL INTERNATIONAL, INC., *London*

For Australasia:
PAUL FLESCH & CO., PTY. LTD., *Melbourne*

For Canada:
M. G. HURTIG LTD., *Edmonton*

This book is published for the Esther Stevens Brazer Guild
of the Historical Society of Early American Decoration, Inc.
by the Charles E. Tuttle Company, Inc., Rutland, Vermont
& Tokyo, Japan with editorial offices at Suido 1-chome,
2–6, Bunkyo-ku, Tokyo, Japan.

Library of Congress Catalog
Card No. 60–8158

International Standard Book
No. 0-8048-0460-5

First edition, 1960
Fourth printing, 1971

Book design and typography by J. Y. Kilpatrick

Manufactured in Japan by
The Charles E. Tuttle Company

To the Members of the
Esther Stevens Brazer Guild of the Historical
Society of Early American Decoration who
are dedicated to the preservation of the art of
ornamentation and to maintaining the standards of the finest early craftsmen.

TABLE OF CONTENTS

LIST OF ILLUSTRATIONS

("Plates" are in color, "Figs.," black-and-white)

FOREWORD

IN AMERICA, the ornamented chairs produced in the late eighteenth and early nineteenth centuries, became extremely popular and remained so for some time, despite the fact that furniture experts seem to have considered them novelties of small importance. These chairs were definitely intended not only for the practical purpose of providing seating facilities, but also as things of beauty, to delight the eye of the beholder. Painted in a great variety of background effects and colors, decorated with gold leaf and either hand-painted with oils or stencilled in bronzes and then profusely striped, they were striking pieces of furniture, when newly finished. Today, with their paint mellowed by time, they are still attractive and deserve the interest that is once more shown in them. Some of them appear to be quite delicately constructed and, as the surfaces that bear the main decorative design have been subjected to much scuffing from contact with the back of the sitter, it is truly amazing that so many fine examples of different varieties, with their ornamentation well preserved, have withstood the years at all, and remain for us to admire and study today.

The ornamented chair has been known generally as the Fancy Chair, a term that has been used to describe the entire group of painted and decorated chairs, ranging from their earliest development in the late Regency and Sheraton periods, through the many so-called *Hitchcock* varieties, to the final Victorian product. We use the designation *Fancy*, however, chiefly in referring to the painted American Sheraton chair.

The researcher, attempting to unearth some facts about the development of the ornamented chair, will find himself involved in tracing style trends in construction details, as well as in decoration and in trying to imagine the personalities of the chairmaker as well as the decorator. Often the same craftsman seems to have done both jobs. Though some information about the chair makers can definitely be gained from old advertisements that touted their wares, little factual knowledge about the decorators comes to light. The only signature the decorator used was the repetition of certain units in his designs or, often, the entire pattern. Much imagination is therefore necessary to piece together his existence, as he wandered from shop to shop.

To further complicate the story of the ornamented chair, we find that few other types of furniture show such definite regional differences in construction, color selection and design. Thus, we have New York leading off in the production of the Sheraton Fancy chair; the New England states producing the many Sheraton Windsors, Hitchcocks and Boston rockers; Pennsylvania offering the bright-hued balloon chairs, some heavier rockers and benches; and the South bringing forth the elegant Baltimore or Lafayette chairs.

A study of the various techniques employed in ornamenting these chairs, clearly shows us how the art of decorating was speeded up as time went by, to make mass production possible, until finally it became obsolete, due possibly to the crudeness to which this craft descended. In the following chapters of our book, we will endeavor to reconstruct this gradual process and show how brass mounts and fine inlay work, used to ornament earlier chairs, gave way to hand-painted motifs, how these were replaced by stencilling and how stencilling passed from beautifully shaded designs, produced by the cutting of many units, to those with no shading, cut in one piece.

The Historical Society of Early American Decoration, Inc. is the custodian of all the research material and photographs collected during the busy lifetime of the late Esther Stevens Brazer and it is our intention to use this material to compile further books on ornamented trays, different types of furniture and accessories and decorated walls and floors. In her lifetime Esther Brazer published her book on "Early American Decoration," in which she told about many of the processes and decorative techniques used by the old-time craftsmen. In this first publication after her death, we have delved deeply into her research material and are presenting many of the photographs of ornamented chairs which she took, as well as some taken by our members, and others from museums in various parts of the country. In a very few cases, the photographs show an original chair which has been authentically restored, for the most part by Mrs. Brazer. Because these are exceptionally fine examples of their type, we have included them.

As our Society is composed of a group of persons enthusiastically engaged in the restoration and reproduction of the designs found on all ornamented furnishings, it is presenting, herewith, largely the view of the decorator. Knowing the colossal amount of time and effort needed to take such a chair properly through its varied decorative processes, and the crafts one must successfully master before being able to do so, we have a tremendous respect for that former decorator and have come to identify ourselves with him in trying to reproduce his effects. We feel that he has been neglected.

In publishing this book, the Society hopes it is not only presenting the story of the ornamented chair in an interesting manner, but that it is opening the way for further research and fact-finding about it and its creator.

MARTHA MULLER, Curator
East Williston, New York

ACKNOWLEDGMENTS

WE WISH to express our sincere gratitude to the many people who have contributed to the research that has made this book possible. Although the photographic material is based on pictures which Mrs. Brazer took over the years and ones that her many pupils and friends contributed, pictures have been added by our authors and each one has done her own research. It has been very difficult to trace many of Mrs. Brazer's photographs. Names were missing and addresses were incomplete, and we regret that we have not been able to give personal recognition for each photograph. Special thanks should go to the museums, historical societies, antique dealers and private collectors who have so graciously given permission to use their pictures; to Mr. N. Grier Parke of Woodstock, Vermont, for the generous contribution of his research material and pictures of the John White Windsor chairs; to the Oldham families in Wellesley Hills, Mass. for permission to use the many pictures of chairs from their collections; and to Miss Esther Oldham for her friendly cooperation in obtaining descriptions of some of these chairs and allowing us to take further pictures. I want to express my personal appreciation for the valuable editorial help our associate member, Catherine Hutter, has given me. She has been an enthusiastic and tireless worker and her professional experience has been invaluable.

ZILLA RIDER LEA
Glens Falls, N.Y.

THE ORNAMENTED CHAIR

Its Development in America

(1700—1890)

CHAPTER I

PLATE 1. *Adam-Hepplewhite Chair. Owned by Elias Hasket Derby in 1796. Unusual variation of seven feathers instead of five. The central plume is painted with a vase of flowers. Brown background.*
Courtesy of Museum of Fine Arts, Boston

OUR ENGLISH HERITAGE

(Japanned English Chairs) 1700—1860

SHIRLEY SPAULDING DE VOE

APANNING began in England in the early 1660's. Samuel Pepys noted in his diary, May 23, 1663, "To Greatorex's, and there he showed me his varnish which he hath invented which appears every bit as good as the Indian."

At the end of the 17th century, the word *japanning* was being used for Oriental lacquer work as well as for the false English product, perhaps because the best Eastern lacquer came from Japan. The home product, when well done, was very popular, due in some measure to the use of red, green, blue and yellow for background colors. These colors were more cheerful in contrast to the somber black and brown of the true product and were in demand for foreign trade. As time passed, the word *japan* came to be used for any painted and varnished article.

The first richly ornamented English chairs were introduced in the first half of the 18th century and were japanned in imitation of Oriental lacquer. Usually known as Queen Anne in style, they had "serpentine vase or fiddle splats enclosed by undulating uprights and shaped to form the user's back." The seat rail, with upholstered seat, was usually rounded in front and supported by cabriole legs ending in club feet *(Figs. 1 and 1a)*. Made of beechwood or deal, they were gessoed and painted red, green or black, then ornamented with *chinoiseries*. These were executed with paint, bronzes and metal leaf and portions of the figures were embossed *(Fig. 2)*.

In the time of George the First (1714–1727) an especially fine cabinet and chair-maker who japanned pieces for export, was Giles Grenday *(Fig. 3)*. Later Thomas Chippendale observed that his own designs for pseudo-lacquer chairs were "very proper for a Lady's Dressing Room, especially if it is hung with 'India' paper." It was the vogue at the time for at least one room in the great houses to be decorated with Chinese wallpaper and furniture made of true Eastern lacquer.

In those days there seemed to exist an indifference to the correct geographical location of far off lands, because the word *India* was the popular term for anything Chinese. It was derived from the East India Company which introduced Oriental products to England.

In the 1760's, the neo-classical or Adam style largely replaced the vogue for Chinese ornament and this resulted in a complete change in design. Adam rooms were treated with soft colors, while stucco or *compo*, as it was called, replaced the dark wood carving and Chinese decoration. Ovals and panels on ceilings and walls were painted with allegorical scenes or cameo-like figures, forerunners of the Flaxman designed Wedgwood panels. Similar panels and medallions, some painted on paper panels and varnished, in proper scale, adorn the white or light colored japanned Adam style chairs *(Figs. 8 and 9)*.

The Adam urn is, perhaps, the most commonly known motif employed by Adam and adapted with paint and brush by artists, but many other motifs were popular, too—for instance, ribbons, anthemion—a honeysuckle motif that remained in use for japanned chairs into the American stencil period—husks, *paterae*, peacock feathers, Prince of Wales feathers, floral and drapery swags, beading, roses, spandrel fans, egg and dart borders, acanthus leaves, fuchsia drops, *amorini*, birds, *guilloche*, vases, and wheat. Designs were copied and repeated by the numerous Italian,

French, and English artists and ornamenters of that day *(Figs. 5–6–7)*.

Painted allegorical scenes are attributed to Angelica Kauffmann and designs with *amorini* to Cipriani. Other skilled artists and ornamenters were Pergolesi, Zucchi, Biagio, Egidio, Rebecca, Callon, Mortimer, William Thomas, Joseph Rose, Mathias Locke and Henry Copeland, who worked in the Chippendale shop.

The japanned chairs of the late 18th century were inexpensive substitutes for carved chairs *(Fig. 16)*. We know them from the Hepplewhite *Guide* and the Sheraton *Drawing Book*. Certain mahogany chairs are illustrated which are pointed out as suitable for japanning, "interspersed with a little gilding. . . ." The painted ornament took the place of the carved ornament, often with a thin shadow brushed at one side to give a dimensional effect and simulate the carving. With the use of native soft woods, these painted chairs provided "genteel furniture at a fraction of the cost."

What was noticeable about the japanned chair was the trail of scorn that followed it, for it was condemned as an imitation of the real thing. In spite of this, japanning endured until the close of the 19th century.

Even more heavily scorned were the *papier-mâché* chairs that were made in Birmingham from about 1850 on. They were an example of a manufactured material substituting for wood and covered with japan, which had hitherto hidden the native woods. The English *papier-mâché* was made of several layers of paper glued together and was similar to millboard. It could be cut or molded into any shape.

At first complete chairs were made of *papier-mâché*, but it was finally found necessary to reinforce them with wood or iron. In some cases chairs in the same style were of wood, with the back panels of *papier-mâché (Fig. 13)*. Purely Victorian in design, the ornament was a mixture of paint, metal leaf and pearl shell or nacre. The use of paint and pearl ornament on furniture was not confined to the Victorian period, as is often erroneously believed. Pearl, which was also introduced from the East, was used with painted ornament on European and English wood furniture in the 17th and 18th centuries.

Groups of flowers, scrolls and arabesques, in the manner of the japanners of the Midlands, were the usual ornamentation of the *papier-mâché* chair. Occasionally one finds a famous land mark depicted. The chair illustrated in Fig. 25 has a painting of Warwick Castle: "You see it from the bridge, shining in the Avon. . . ." Another favorite scene for *papier-mâché* painting was Windsor Castle.

The soft wood most commonly used on these early English chairs was beech, which remained popular in spite of comments such as Evelyn's, "The more vulgar beech subject to worm, weak and unsightly." It was plentiful and cheap and in the early *walnut period*, 1660–1745, beech chairs were carved, painted or stained to represent more expensive woods. The soft woods, beech and deal, were gessoed to provide a smooth surface for the well-crafted pseudo-lacquer chair. This type suffered in the American climate and centrally heated rooms, which caused the gesso and embossing to crack and chip. Few have survived, due to their susceptibility to worm and dry climate.

While on the subject of wood, it should be mentioned that English and American birch were used for furniture in the late 18th century. That American birch was satisfactory for japanning we know from a 19th century coachmaker who wrote, "American birch works easily with the plane and yields a beautifully smooth surface which does not show the smallest particle of grain beneath the most delicate paint work. ..." Both English and American birch were used for "carcass" work as well, especially where the front surfaces were veneered with satinwood.

In the revival of Pompeian and Roman classicism, the choice of light colors brought about the use of satinwood for furniture. The best came from the East India Islands and was used as a veneer, often inlaid with designs of exotic woods such as Amboyna, or padouk, ebony and olive wood. The important chairmaker selected the wood with care from a stock of well seasoned timber which he kept in his own yard. The plain surfaces of satinwood furniture were ornamented with some of the finest painting of the 18th century and in some instances the brush imitated marquetry.

Another feature of the Adam period was the use of cane, which was reintroduced after a lapse of about thirty years. "Caning cabinet work is now more in use than it ever was known to be at any former period," Sheraton wrote *(Fig. 13)*.

Cane chairs first appeared in the early part of the reign of Charles the Second, (1660) arriving by way of Holland and the Dutch East India Company. The demand for them increased due to their cleanliness, comfort and resiliency and because they cost less than upholstered chairs. A special skill was needed, particularly for the graduated cane work in the round or oval backs of the Adam-Hepplewhite chairs. Added comfort was assured by the use of a "fine, thick hair squab," placed on the cane seat *(Fig. 19)*. Down or feathers were also used to fill the squabs, as the plump, loose cushions were called.

Upholstered seats were "stuff'd over the rails with Brass Nails in one or two rows and sometimes the Nails are done to imitate fretwork." Others were upholstered within the rail and all were stuffed with hair, wool or linen flocks. A method for making a springy hair stuffing was described by the previously quoted coachmaker, as follows: "Horse hair forcibly twisted into a peculiar curl, baked in an oven to fix it, was used for an elastic stuffing."

The materials most commonly used for covering the seats and cushions were serge, silk damask, printed cotton, chintz and horse hair. The latter was not always the gloomy black of the late Victorian period *(Fig. 12)* "but was plain, striped or chequered etc. at pleasure."

It is impossible to draw a sharp line of distinction between the designs of the japanned chairs of the period. There were many pattern books which were available to all chair makers, and they drew freely from them, often incorporating their own ideas. Therefore to simplify matters they are loosely categorized as Adam-Chippendale, Adam-Hepplewhite and Adam-Sheraton, according to their chief characteristics. Other cabinet and chair makers of note were Edwards and Darley, Thomas Johnson, Robert Manwaring, Ince and Mayhew and George Seddon, "one of the most eminent cabinet makers of London;" his firm was later known as Seddon Sons and Shackleton *(Fig. 10)*.

Robert Adam's death in 1792 marked the close of a great period, and the start of the Regency style, which is understood to cover 1800–1820, although the Prince of Wales was not made Regent until 1811. The Prince, later George the Fourth, was largely responsible for the revival of the Chinese style which he used in the rooms of the Royal Pavilion at Brighton.

Chairs with horizontal lines were favored, with "saber-shaped legs, arms set high on the back uprights, giving a characteristic high-shouldered appearance." *(Figs. 20 and 21)*. Regency chairs were hand grained or japanned black and ornamented mainly with gilt *chinoiseries*. Japanners were once more supplying chairs of an "inferior mode" by imitating the better woods and gilding to simulate the Birmingham brass ornaments which were in vogue for the finer chairs. Gilt stripes replaced the thin brass inlaid strips and gilt was used on open fretwork, on the finials of chair posts and on the knobs on "bamboo" turnings in Sheraton influenced chairs *(See Figs. 22 and 23)*.

That any of the chairs described in this chapter were made in America seems questionable. While there were some fine craftsmen making mahogany chairs in the 18th century, such craftsmen would have needed specialists to ornament their chairs and probably looked down on a japanned product. The richly ornamented chair of the Adam-Hepplewhite type demanded an especially skilled ornamenter with a finesse which has never been equalled on American *Fancies*. In the humble "home industry" here, small shops were the first answer to the English suppression of American manufacture, and they were poor. In the period of which we are speaking, this country was being kept by Britain on a strictly agricultural level. England still had a monopoly on all manufactured goods. American japanners had to import their supplies and few of them had cash. When the Revolution ended, money was scarce and business here was being transacted mainly by the barter system. Only the richer citizens in prosperous areas could afford to buy the more elegant English chairs. Orders were placed with dealers and cabinet makers in this country, who passed them on to England. The finished product was delivered to the American buyer after the necessary time had elapsed, and time was needed—not only for shipping, but for the manufacturing itself, since everything was done by hand. There were no molding machines or circular saws for chair making. The cabinet maker then sold the imported article with his own products. This is what may have led to the confusion which credits American chairmakers with some of our finest English imports *(Figs. 14 and 15)*.

It was in the first quarter of the 19th century that American Sheraton or *Fancy* chairs were being made and japanned in quantity in this country. Simple and naive in comparison with English Sheratons, they had noticeable features and traits derived mainly from the English Adam and Sheraton type of ornament. The following chapter introduces them to you.

GLOSSARY

ACANTHUS An architectural ornament adapted for furniture.

AMORINI Cupids.

ANTHEMION Greek stylized honeysuckle.

ARABESQUE An intricate pattern of interlaced lines.

CANE CHAIR A chair with a seat and sometimes a back of tightly woven cane.

CHINOISERIES Chinese decoration.

CONVOLUTE A coil or whorl.

DEAL A slice cut from a log of timber (fir or pine) and cut into standard lengths.

FANCY CHAIRS OR FANCIES A term used in New England for a japanned and ornamented chair popular from about 1810.

FLOCKS A material consisting of the coarse tufts and refuse of wool or cotton or linen torn to pieces...used for stuffing upholstery.

GESSO A preparation of plaster and glue for use as a surface for painting.

GILT Generally means gold leaf or Dutch metal in the furniture trade.

GUILLOCHE An ornament in the form of two or more bands twisting over each other repeatedly. Similar to a cable but with a more circular twist.

JAPANNING The art of producing a highly varnished surface on wood, metal or *papier-mâché*, plain or ornamented.

PATERAE Any flat round ornament in bas relief. A rosette, usually placed in the block above the leg of a chair.

SABER LEG A sharply curved leg in the classical style.

FIG. 1. *Black japanned pseudo-lacquer chair with embossed Chinese ornamentation. Cabriole leg, undulating uprights and vase splat. c. 1740.*
Courtesy of the Philadelphia Museum of Art

FIG. 1a. *Side view of chair in Fig. 1*

FIG. 2. *Beechwood pseudo-lacquer chair. c. 1700. Green and gold on red japan. Cabriole leg, pied de biche (doe's foot) or donkey's hoof termination. Without a stretcher.*
Courtesy of the Victoria and Albert Museum, London. Crown copyright.

FIG. 3. *Painted in imitation of Chinese lacquer. Beech. 18th century. Bears original label of "Grendey."*
Courtesy of the Metropolitan Museum of Art. Gift of Louis J. Boury, 1937.

FIG. 4. *Adam-Hepplewhite chair, one of a set of 24, bought in Philadelphia by Elias Hasket Derby in 1796. Ivory color ground, rich green bow-knot, green leaves, red rose buds, dark brown feathering.*
Museum of Fine Arts, Boston

FIG. 5. *Similar to Fig. 4. Painted beechwood. Grey-white ground, blue-grey stripes and acanthus. Red and yellow bows. Natural color peacock feathers. Square, tapered legs, spade foot. c. 1795.*
Museum of Fine Arts, Boston

FIG. 6. *Pale green background. Bird and flowers in natural colors. Rosette over leg and bow on front of seat in blue. Leaf forms and turnings gold. Formerly E. S. Brazer collection. On loan at Farmer's Museum, Cooperstown, New York.*

FIG. 7. *Similar type chair, c. 1796, showing six feathers in oval. Dark brown background. Flowers and leaves in natural colors.*
Courtesy of the Metropolitan Museum of Art. Gift of Mrs. J. Insley Blair, 1947.

FIG. 8. *Adam Period. Mahogany, painted black and ivory with decorative detail in color. c. 1780–85. Courtesy of Victoria and Albert Museum, London*

FIG. 9. *Armchair with lyre back. Creamy white background, blue swags and bows. Green vines with red berries around back oval. Green leaf-forms on lower part of lyre, also on legs. Gilt turnings. c. 1780. Present owner unknown*

FIG. 10. *Painted satinwood Adam-Hepplewhite chair. Cane seat with squab. Shield back. This armchair corresponds exactly with a set of chairs supplied by Seddon, Sons and Schackleton to D. Tupper of Guernsey. c. 1790. Victoria and Albert Museum, London*

FIG. 11. *Pair of Adam-Hepplewhite armchairs. Japanned beechwood. Painted urn and flowers. c. 1790. Victoria and Albert Museum, London*

FIG. 12. *Hepplewhite Adam period. Beechwood, painted or japanned in colors. Splat in the form of Prince of Wales feathers. c. 1790. Courtesy of Victoria and Albert Museum, London*

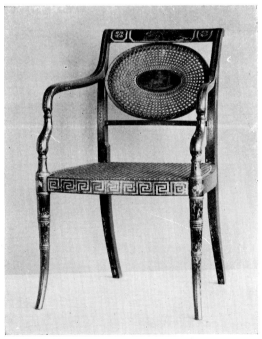

FIG. 13. *Adam Regency period. Beechwood, japanned in black and gold. In the center of the caned oval, a medallion of pâper maché. Painted in gresaille. c. 1800. Courtesy of Victoria and Albert Museum, London*

FIG. 14. *Adam period chair. Label says, "Made by John Seymour, for the Hon. Nathaniel Silsbee, about 1790. When he built his house." Possibly imported from England by John Seymour.*
Courtesy of Mrs. B. K. Little

FIG. 15. *Similar type chair. Blue "Wedgewood" vase design in center splat. Note stretchers in both these chairs.*
Formerly owned by E. S. Brazer

FIG. 16. *Adam-Hepplewhite period chair. Design painted in imitation of carving, in colors on mottled brown background. Adam ornamentation. 1780–90.*
Owner unknown

FIG. 17. *Adam-Hepplewhite bench. "Benches are chairs doub led and trebled." Painted ornamentation on back and arms.*
Possibly American.
Present owner unknown

FIG. 18. *Adam-Hepplewhite bench. Painted ornamentation.*
Owner unknown

FIG. 19. *Settee. Japanned beechwood. Caned. c. 1790.*
Courtesy of Victoria and Albert Museum, London

FIG. 20. *Regency period chair. Open gilded fretwork and chinoiseries. High-shouldered look. Saber legs. Victoria and Albert Museum, London*

FIG. 21. *Regency period chair. Turned beechwood, japanned in black and gold. c. 1800. Victoria and Albert Museum, London*

FIG. 22. *Example of English Sheraton chair which influenced the American Sheraton. Child's high chair. Early 19th century. Painted ornamentation. Bamboo turnings.*
Victoria and Albert Museum, London

FIG. 23. *American Sheraton chair showing English Sheraton influence. Painted and gilded.*
Courtesy of the Metropolitan Museum of Art. Bequest of Maria P. James, 1911.

FIG. 24. *Mid-Victorian bench. Ornamentation in pearl shell and paint. Gold convolutes and arabesques.*
Victoria and Albert Museum, London

FIG. 25. *Mid-Victorian chair. Wood and papier-mâché. Painting of Warwick Castle. Courtesy of the Victoria and Albert Museum, London*

PLATE 2. *Sheraton Fancy armchair, pale cream yellow, decorated with a landscape on the top slat and a design of roses on the front seat. 1795–1800.*
An authentic restoration from the Oldham collection

CHAPTER II

OUR FANCY CHAIRS ADOPT SHERATON DETAILS

EMILIE RICH UNDERHILL

FANCY CHAIRS enjoyed great popularity in America throughout the first half of the 19th century. They were the offspring of the late English Sheraton chairs, with the ornamentation showing much of the classic Adam influence. In almost every instance they are simplifications of the more ornate and elegant English examples. Sheraton chairs and the Sheraton influence found their way to America as most European art styles did—by the import of the article itself, by individuals bringing furniture with them when they emigrated or bringing articles of furniture home with them from their travels abroad. And then, of course, the chairmaker brought the Sheraton style influence with him when he moved from the Old Country to the New.

In 1797, for instance, William Challen arrived in this country from London, armed with all the latest chair design books. His advertisement in New York that year read, "William Challen, Fancy Chairmaker from London, makes all sorts of dyed, japanned, wangee and bamboo chairs, settees, etc., and every article in the Fancy Chair line, executed in the neatest manner and after the newest and most approved London patterns."

The Fancy Chair was manufactured in rural areas as well as in the large cities. Some were made of maple, others of beech or light, soft wood which lent itself so well to japanning. Seats were mainly of rush or flag. We find later types with the seat made of wood. Cane was more rarely used because of the expense of importing it from England.

The early Fancy Chairs were costly and found their way only into the homes of the well-to-do. As business flourished and the demand for them became more urgent, manufacturers produced them in such phenomenal quantities, often selling them by the dozen, that they came within the reach of everyone. They were seen in dining rooms, parlors, bedrooms and, commercially, in tap rooms and hotels. They gained great popularity as furnishings for dining salons, lounges and cabins on the River Steamboats, where they acquired the name "Steamboat Fancies." They were shipped to the Southern States and, later, export to the West Indies became important.

To appreciate these pieces fully, one should have some knowledge of Sheraton and his fundamental characteristics of style. He was born in England, in Stockton-on-Tees, in 1751, and he learned the rudiments of cabinet making as a youth, in his father's shop. But his fame rests solely in his designs, for little or nothing is known of anything he actually constructed. Thus the chairs we are accustomed to calling *Sheraton chairs* are not of actual Sheraton construction but those influenced by his designs.

That he was an inventive genius is borne out in some of his unusual ideas for design, such as an ottoman with "heating urn" underneath the seat, folding beds, a table with a concealed step ladder and a couch which could be changed into a table. But above all he was a painstaking and meticulous draftsman.

We have much to be grateful for in the execution of his drawings. They were handled with infinite care. He was a stickler for the geometrics and perspective of his layouts, fastidious in his details and gave explicit directions for following them. The *Drawing Book* was intended as a book of designs for the use of cabinet makers, not as a catalogue of pieces for sale. In 1803 he published *The*

Cabinet Dictionary and was in the process of writing *The Cabinet-Maker, Upholsterer and General Artist's Encyclopedia*, when he died.

Delicacy, refinement and elegance are salient characteristics of his style. We find straight lines and square backs giving an effect of slenderness. Banisters or diagonal lattice backs are typical. Two or three horizontal rungs are joined by small balls, giving strength to the chair's construction. A horizontal rail, slightly above the seat, supports banisters or a central splat. Arms are high and often extend from just below the top rail, giving the chair what one might call a "Regency look." Sometimes the arm supports are vase shaped and attached to the outside of the seat rail. Legs are straight, slim and tapering—reeded, fluted or plain. Bamboo turnings were seen in chairs influenced by the Windsor chair.

In later periods, the slender top rail becomes wider, slats are sometimes cut out in fret work. We find round top rails, reeded or with turnings, on each side of a central bolster. Stretchers and posts are shaped and flattened in front to permit decoration. Legs are splayed at the base.

In Sheraton's so-called "decadent period," which he felt obliged to adopt because of popular demand and for economic reasons, his designs are influenced by the ponderous Napoleonic or Empire period and have to be seen to be believed! Chair backs take on the forms of animals or serpents. One drawing of his shows an anchor with twined rope composing the back, while dolphins support the seat. Chair legs and posts terminate in grotesque animal heads with carved, furry manes running down the sides. This period is mentioned simply because it existed, but it should be

dismissed as not worthy of the creations of the great artist that was Sheraton. That its influence made itself felt on the American Sheraton chair is demonstrated by Fig. 56.

Sheraton's famous *Cabinet-maker and Upholsterer's Drawing Book*, which did perhaps more than anything else to establish his style, was composed of several parts, the first of which was published in 1791. The preface, with its arrogant and uncharitable criticism of Chippendale, Hepplewhite and his contemporaries, gives us insight into the bitterness and frustration of a man who, in spite of his genius, was doomed to die in poverty. Sheraton was contemptuous in his references to their drawings, particularly Hepplewhite, yet he seemed to feel no qualms about borrowing extravagantly from them. Comparison of the designs of each prove this beyond a doubt. Nevertheless, from the ideas that came to him from these borrowings, he brought forth a distinctive style of his own.

His drawings appear in the third part of his book. They are dated 1792–1793, so could not have been copied in this country much before 1794–1795. This gives us a definite date on which to establish the age of our Sheraton influenced Fancy Chairs. Otherwise we have very little to go by. It was not the custom in America, during the early period of the Fancy Chair, to label furniture. Occasionally a business card might be attached to a piece, but throughout years of usage and changing hands, these have been lost or destroyed. Thus it has become almost impossible to make a positive identification of the maker.

Of course a study of old advertisements can be a great help to us. An advertisement in New York City in 1802 reads: "Fancy Chairs and Cornices. William Palmer, No. 2 Nassau

Street, near Federal Hall, has for sale a large assortment of elegant well-made and highly finished, black and gold, etc., Fancy Chairs with cane and rush bottoms. . . . Old chairs repaired, regilt, etc., at lowest price and agreeably to any pattern. Ornamental painting and gilding neatly executed."

In New York City in 1810, "Paterson & Dennis, No. 54 John Street, inform their friends and the public that they have now on hand a large and very elegant assortment of Fancy Chairs of the newest patterns and finished in superior style. Elegant white, coquelicot*, green, etc., and gilt drawing-room chairs, with cane and rush seats, together with a handsome assortment of dining and bedroom chairs, etc."

In 1812, the New York public read an advertisement: "Asa Holden, 32 Broad Street, has a superb assortment of highly finished Fancy Chairs, such as double and single cross, fret, chain, gold, ball and spindle back, with cane and rush seats, etc., of the latest and most fashionable patterns. The cane seats are warranted to be American made, which are known to be much superior to any imported from India."

Again in New York City in 1817, "Wheaton and Davies, Fancy Chair manufacturers have removed from 15 Bowery to 153 Fulton Street, opposite St. Paul's Church, where they offer for sale an elegant assortment of curled maple, painted, ornamented, landscaped sewing and rocking chairs. . . ."

Some of the finest examples of Sheraton Fancies came from Baltimore in the first quarter of the 19th century. Working there were William Camp, John Findlay, John Staples and Robert Fisher. (One of his chairs

* coquelicot—a poppy color (Webster's Dictionary)

is pictured on p. 209, vol. 1. of *American Antique Furniture* by Edgar G. Miller.) Alex Ingram painted and decorated chairs in Baltimore.

In Salem, Mass., Samuel McIntire, the famous designer of houses, turned his hand to making some of the finest Sheraton style furniture in the United States. And it was in Salem that the chairs for the yacht, *Cleopatra's Barge* were made *(Fig. 32)*. The story of that famous ship, although definitely a digression, is too fascinating to be passed over with a mere illustration of her Fancy Chairs. She was built for Capt. George Crowninshield in Salem in 1816 by Retire Becket in his shipyard at the foot of Derby Street. She was 83 feet at the water line with a 191 ton displacement. Rigged as a brigantine, she was painted in gay decor with herringbone diagonals on her port side and horizontal stripes of many colors on the starboard side. A wooden figurehead graced her prow and on the deck was a life-size statue of an Indian warrior in war paint.

No expense was spared in her construction. She cost $50,000 to build, a sizable sum in those days, and this did not include her furnishings. The saloon or main cabin was 19′ by 20′ and panelled in polished, inlaid mahogany. There were velvet draperies, gilt eagle mirrors and a magnificent chandelier hung from the ceiling. Two enormous settees, 11 feet long, with backs composed of five lyre splats and upholstered in crimson velvet, stood against the wall. The sideboard was laden with an especially designed silver service and the cupboards were filled with superb china and glassware which had been made to order.

Capt. Crowninshield was one of five brothers who commanded ships out of Salem. *Cleopatra's Barge*, which he originally named

Car of Concordia, was built as a pleasure yacht and was the first as such to cross the Atlantic. He made only one cruise aboard her, and a mysterious cruise it was. He took her to the Mediterranean. Rumor had it that he had gone to rescue Napoleon from St. Helena and bring him back to America. He went armed with many letters of introduction to prominent persons, and when he stopped at Elba and later visited Napoleon's family in Rome and accepted many choice gifts from them, the British Navy set out to keep an eye on his movements until he sailed for home. He died of a heart attack aboard his beloved yacht in Salem Harbor, scarcely a month after his return.

After his death, *Cleopatra's Barge* was dismantled and sold at auction into the merchant service running to South America. The lavish furnishings were divided among Capt. Crowninshield's brothers and sisters. Later she became the private yacht of King Kamehameha II of the Hawaiian Islands, who renamed her *Haaheo o Hawaii*, Pride of Hawaii. She was wrecked on the Island of Kauai in 1824.

The chair illustrated in Fig. 32 was one of the set made for the dining salon. The top slat is decorated with a descriptive scene—there was a different scene on each chair. A row of tiny stars across the middle rail is said to be the trade mark of the decorator. Note the detail of leaves near the top of the legs.

In the meantime Pittsburgh had become the home of Fancy Chair mass production. Graham & Montgomery of that city made tremendous shipments to the Western Territory, and the firm of White & Hamilton supplied the Ohio River Steamboats and hotels with chairs similar to the Hitchcock. Their output was said to exceed that of the Hitch-

cock factory at its peak. Cincinnati was another important Fancy Chair center. The names of Samuel Sibles, Frances Harrison and Joel Perkins appear in advertisements. John Wilson was a chair painter as well as a manufacturer here.

These are but a few of the names associated with the trade. So popular did the Fancy Chair become that the manufacturers divorced themselves from the cabinet makers and formed their own societies and advertised as "Fancy Chair Makers." One of the most important men in the Fancy Chair industry, John Cowperthwaite of 4 Chatham Square, New York City, became president of the Master Chair Maker Society. A civic parade, marking the opening of the Erie Canal, saw him leading the 3rd division which consisted of 200 Fancy Chair makers.

It is interesting to learn the price some of these chairs brought. In 1818, Bruce and Dean of Broad Street, New York, advertised Fancy Chairs of excellent workmanship at $5.00 and $7.50 each. In 1820, Henry Hubon of Salem, Mass. sent a bill of $35.00 for 8 Fancy Chairs. (Bill reproduced in the Essex Institute publication, *Artists and Craftsmen of Essex County, Mass.* Compiled by Henry W. Belknap. Nov. 22, 1820, lists "8 Fancy Chairs—$35.00.") In 1824, Silas A. Nichols, New Haven, Conn. received $30.00 for 12 curly maple chairs of fine quality. (Bill of sale on record, dated New Haven, June 15, 1824. "Mrs. H. H. Edwards, Bo't of S. A. Nichols, 12 curly maple chairs $2.50–$30.00. To varnishing sofa and repairing chair—.50. $30.50. Pay rec'd Silas A. Nichols.") And in 1834, Tweed & Bonner asked $18.00 per dozen for good chairs. Today these chairs are assessed for their historic and antique value.

The day of the true cabinet and chair maker has gone. In many cases hand-crafted copies would cost more than the antique itself.

The most sought after Sheraton Fancy Chair is that of early design (1800–10) with the square seat framed by a narrow band, trim rounded legs and posts with gilt finials. See Figs. 1, 2 and 7 for beautifully decorated examples. These early chairs were ornamented with the paint brush, with the turnings in gilt. The early white chairs were usually striped with burnt umber. This same type chair would have delicately turned spindles or the uprights or banister would be shaped to form panels, urns and medallions, a last reflection of the Adam period. The cross-bars and stretchers were similarly shaped.

While many of these features remain in the later examples, we soon find fretwork and cross-bands introduced in the backs, *bamboo* turnings on the stretchers, legs, spindles and posts (1810–20). Seats begin to be rounded, with wider bands. Heavier top slats appear.

Ornamentation on the early English Sheraton Fancy Chair generally took the form of carving or inlay. When this was replaced by painting in the American Sheraton Fancy, we find the same cameo-like panels, swags, urns, plumes, shells, cornucopias, leaves, and fruit. But as what we might term "the Adam feeling," with its light colored or white backgrounds and decoration of urns, draperies and swags, loses favor, we see dark colors becoming popular. Dark greens, browns and vermilion take the place of the lighter, more delicate background. With the rounded seat we often find pumpkin yellow used. Oak leaves and grapes, flower groups and shells are painted on the later broad panels and slats. The gold striping is much wider. Sometimes we find two decorated slats instead of one at the back of the chair. The legs take on aspects of Empire or Directoire construction. The black-on-red graining, which became popular in the Empire period and with the Hitchcock chair, is used as a background and is frequently ornamented with stencils, although generally metal leaf was used on the turnings. We begin to find scenic paintings, as in the Cleopatra's Barge chair, on the top slats.

With these features in mind, let us study some of the chairs illustrated.

SHERATON FANCY

Banister backs. Horizontal rail slightly above seat, supporting banisters or central splat: Figs. 1 through 9, 15, 49, 50.

Diagonal lattice backs: Figs. 10, 11, 20, 26, 27.

Horizontal rungs (2 or 3) *sometimes joined by small balls:* Figs. 12, 13, 14, 16, 17, 18, 25, 29 through 37, 39, 41, 42, 44, 45, 47, 51, 53, 54.

Slender top rail becomes wider in later designs: Fig. 20.

Arms high, extend from just below top rail: Figs. 21, 23, 24, 29, 33 through 37, 43, 51.

Arm supports often vase shaped, attached to side of seat rail: Figs. 9, 11, 23, 24c, 29, 33, 34, 35, 40, 43.

Legs straight, tapering, slender, reeded, fluted or plain: Figs. 1 through 20, 23, 24, 26, 27, 36, 37, 39, 40, 41, 43 through 47, 49, 50.

Horizontal splats sometimes *cut out* (later period): Figs. 19, 23, 24, 25, 28, 33, 34, 45, 52, 55.

Round top rail, reeded or with turnings each side of central bolster (later period): Figs. 53, 54, 55.

Stiles flattened on front side to allow for decoration (later period): Figs. 2, 10, 11, 16, 18, 20, 23 through 35, 38, 39, 40, 42, 44 through 49, 52, 53, 54, 55.

Stretchers shaped to permit decoration (later period): Figs. 1 through 9, 13, 14, 15, 20, 23, 24, 26, 27, 36, 37, 40, 45, 48, 49.

Legs splayed at base (later period): Figs. 21, 22, 25, 28 through 35, 38, 41, 48, 51 through 55.

Bamboo turnings. See Chapter I. Fig. 23.

FIG. 1. *Yellow Sheraton Fancy chair. c. 1800–*
10. From George Rea Curven Estate, formerly
owned by Esther Stevens Brazer.
Courtesy of Essex Institute, Salem, Mass.

FIG. 2. *Side chair with acorn finials, painted in pale*
buff. Urn and peacock feathers show Adam influence.
Middle and side banisters and bands in gold leaf.
Striping in burnt umber. c. 1810–15.
Formerly owned by Mrs. Arthur Oldham

FIG. 3. *Early chairs, about 1800. Decorated with swags, urn and grapes. Note the decoration at*
top of legs.
Formerly owned by E. S. Brazer

FIG. 4. *Sheraton chairs with gold leaf and painted ornamentation.*
Courtesy of Mrs. Lois Greer

FIG. 5. *About 1810. Present owner unknown.*

FIG. 6. *Dark green chair. Harlow and Howland, Decorators, Boston, Mass.*

FIG. 7. *Fancy Sheraton with acorn finials. Painted dark chocolate brown. Middle banister urn-shaped. Grape decorations on banisters in gold leaf. c. 1810–15. Formerly owned by Mrs. John E. Oldham*

FIG. 8. *Similar type side chair. Present owner unknown.*

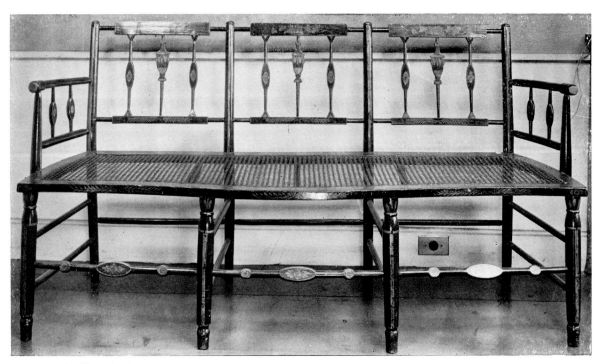

FIG. 9. *Note the classic urn ana laurel leaf motif, and the small, flattened panel decoration on the stretchers. Formerly owned by Alfred Uhler, Concord, Mass.*

FIG. 10. *Brown chair decorated in gold leaf, white and black. Note the classic swags on stiles and legs. Formerly owned by E. S. Brazer*

FIG. 11. *Arm chair. Cane seat. Gold leaf decoration. Present owner unknown*

FIG. 12. *Adaptation of both banister and rail back. c. 1820. Present owner unknown*

FIGS. 13 & 14. *Charming adaptation of both the banister and rail back. Decorated with formal crossed feathers and simple conventional motif.*
Formerly owned by Mrs. Katherine Bryer

FIG. 15. *Fancy chair ornamented in gold on black.*
Present owner unknown

FIG. 16. *Painted dark red and decorated with greyish white grapes and leaves. Tendrils in scarlet.*
Formerly owned by E. S. Brazer

FIG. 17. *Similar type armchair from the Oldham Collection.*

FIG. 18. *Present owner unknown.*

FIG. 19. *Formerly owned by E. S. Brazer.*

FIG. 20. *Side chair painted white and decorated with freehand bronze and gold. Note the reeded legs and stiles.*
Courtesy of Mrs. Norman J. Bruen

FIGS. 21 & 22. *Sheraton Fancy armchair and side chair, made in New York. City, 1820. Vermilion, with brass mounts and gold leaf decoration.*
Courtesy of the Metropolitan Museum of Art, Rogers Fund, 1945

FIG. 23. *Fretwork reminiscent of the English Regency period. Classic fluted leg. Decoration in gold. 1820.*
Courtesy of Museum of the City of New York

FIGS. 24a, b, & c. *Part of a set with landscape panels, each different. Notice the scenic panels on the seat fronts. Present owner unknown*

FIG. 25. *Exceptionally fine freehand bronze decoration of grapes and leaves in greenish bronze, outlined and detailed in black. Courtesy of Mrs. Edward Dierauer*

FIG. 26. *Pale green Sheraton Fancy, decorated in freehand bronze and gold. Popular "leaping deer" pattern. Present owner unknown*

FIG. 27. *Lattice-back Sheraton Fancy, gold leaf decoration. c. 1815. Present owner unknown*

FIG. 28. *Painted turquoise blue, showing free-hand bronze pattern in black and silver. c. 1815.*
Present owner unknown

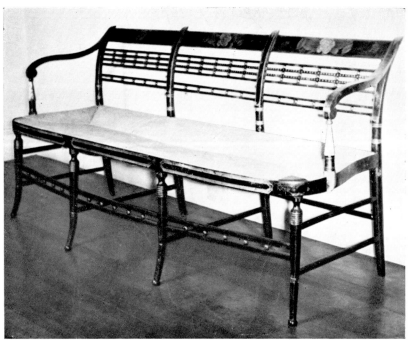

FIGS. 29 & 30. *Side chair and settee with tortoise shell grained background. Top slat decorated with large, stencilled gold leaf flower, shaded with umber. Leaves are stencilled with bronze powder, veins painted in black. Balls, bands, and turnings in gold leaf, striping in yellow. Row of stars across the two middle rails are said to be the trademark of the decorator. c. 1800—Cesinsky.*
Oldham Collection

FIG. 31. *19th century Sheraton Fancy. Rush seat painted. Stencilling and freehand bronze decoration. Courtesy of the Metropolitan Museum of Art. Bequest of Mrs. Maria P. James, 1911.*

FIG. 32. *One of a set of dining room chairs made for "Cleopatra's Barge," built for Capt. George Crowninshield at Salem, Mass. Courtesy of Essex Institute, Salem, Mass. Now in the Peabody Museum of Salem.*

FIG. 33. *Freehand bronze and gold leaf decoration. c. 1820. Present owner unknown*

FIG. 34. *Similar type set of Sheraton Fancies. 1 armchair. 5 side chairs. Freehand bronze and gold leaf decoration. Note unusual treatment of stiles. 1824.*
Present owner unknown

FIG. 35. *Curly maple chairs, decorated with simple gold leaf bands and turnings. Sold for $2.50 each in 1824. Very fine examples of restraint in ornamentation, which is carried out in striping only. Bill of sale on record.*
Courtesy of Charles W. Lyons, New York City.

FIG. 36. *Decorated with conventional motifs.*
Present owner unknown

FIG. 37. *Sheraton Fancy armchair, pale cream yellow, decorated with a landscape on the top slat and a design of roses on the front seat. 1795–1800.*
An authentic restoration by Mrs. Brazer from the Oldham collection

FIG. 38. *Red and black grained side chair with grape decoration and gold leaf bands.*
Present owner unknown

FIG. 39. *Side chair decorated with gold leaf beehive and cornucopia.*
Present owner unknown

FIGS. 40 & 40a. *Freehand bronze and gold leaf decoration, accents and striping in black. Present owner unknown*

FIG. 41. *Small panel at top decorated with leaf decoration.*
Collection of Mrs. Arthur Oldham

FIG. 42. *Ornamentation in gold leaf. Note graceful swags on top of stiles. 1815–20. Present owner unknown*

FIG. 43.   *Sheraton type folding bedstead or settee. Pale yellow background. Decoration: etched gold leaf and freehand bronze, with black painted details. Black striping.*
Courtesy of Mr. & Mrs. Walter W. Stokes

FIG. 44.   *Ornamentation showing stencilling combined with gold leaf.*
Present owner unknown

FIG. 45.   *Scroll back chair. Its design, scrolls in gold leaf, is typical of the date, c. 1810.*

FIG. 46. *Late Sheraton Empire. Has the appearance of a tortoise-shell background. Stencilled decoration.*
Courtesy, Essex Institute, Salem, Mass.

FIG. 47. *Sheraton Empire side chair, stencilled decoration.*
Collection of Mrs. John E. Oldham

FIG. 48. *Late Sheraton Fancy, 1815–20, with three back slats graduating in size.*
Owned by Mrs. George M. Van Duser. Courtesy Florence E. Wright.

FIG. 49. *Side chair painted oyster white. Arrow spindles customarily run from top slat to seat.*
Formerly owned by Mrs. John E. Oldham

FIG. 50. *Window seat, very popular in Robert Adam's time. Probably American, with strong English feeling. Classic ornamentation: urn, drapery, Greek key and paterae. Present owner unknown*

FIG. 51. *Animal and scenic decoration covering the entire top slat was very popular around 1815–20. Courtesy of Mrs. Clark's Shop, New Bedford, Mass.*

FIG. 52. *Dolphin chair. Dark green background. Top slat shows elaborate scene in natural colors. The dolphins, shell and small motifs are gold. This chair had a rush seat.*
Courtesy of Mrs. Maxwell Riddle, Ravenna, Ohio

FIG. 53. *Grained thin black over vermilion making "tortoiseshell" background. Pillow-top with etched gold leaf ornamentation. Forerunner of the "Hitchcock" chair.*
Courtesy of Shirley S. De Voe

FIG. 54. *Yellow side chair with simple decoration in gold leaf and green painted leaf sprays.*
Present owner unknown

FIG. 55. *Sheraton type, cut-out slat with pillow top. Scrolls and small basket of fruit on center slat are gold leaf.*
Courtesy of Miss Fanny Benedict, Warwick, N. Y.

FIG. 56. *Early 19th century side chair. Greek revival. Painted and gilded. Again we find the "leaping deer" pattern. (see Fig. 26).*
Courtesy Metropolitan Museum of Art, Rogers Fund, 1954.

SEYMOUR WATROUS.

INFORMS the public that he has lately commenced the Cabinet and Chair Making business in Central Row, No. 6, directly south of the State-House Square, at the sign of the "Hartford Cabinet and Chair Ware-House," where he is manufacturing from the best materials and by experienced workmen, CABINET FURNITURE and CHAIRS of every description, which he will warrant to be finished in a style equal if not superior to any, and will sell on as reasonable terms as can be purchased at any other Store in this city, or in the city of New-York.

Old Chairs repaired, painted and re-gilt so as to look nearly as well as new.

WANTED IMMEDIATELY,

One Journeyman Chair Maker, and two young lads from the country, fifteen or sixteen years of age, as Apprentices to the Chair making business.

Hartford, March 2, 1824.   1y75

FIG. 57. *Advertisement from the Hartford Courant, March 2, 1824.*

NEW-YORK ANNUAL ADVERTISER.

FANCY AND WINDSOR
CHAIR MANUFACTORY.

THOMAS ASH,

No. 33 JOHN-STREET,

Having, by the death of his father, succeeded to the long established and well known manufactory of Fancy and Windsor Chairs, takes occasion to solicit, from the public, a continuance of the favor swhich have been so long and so liberally bestowed upon his predecessor. He has already in employ a number of the very best and most tasteful workmen, and is ready to receive orders, which will be executed with fidelity and promptness. Those persons who may please to favour him with their commands, may rely upon a strict attention to the execution of their orders. On hand, an assortment of Chairs, both Fancy and Windsor, of the newest fashions, and suited for domestic use or the foreign market.

FIG. 58. *From the New York City Directory, 1817.*

CHAPTER III

PLATE 3. *John White Windsor Chairs.*
Courtesy Mr. N. Grier Parke, Woodstock, Vermont

SHERATON INFLUENCES
THE WINDSOR CHAIR

BERNICE M. DRURY

HERE IS an oft-told tale, vouched for by some, disputed by others, of how this common chair received its royal name. *They* say that one of the royal Georges, seeing a chair of this type in a farmhouse near the castle, so greatly admired the beauty of its simple lines that he brought it to the attention of the court and made it fashionable. Soon Windsor chairs could be found in kitchen, dining room and parlor, in bars, courtrooms and educational institutions. That they are still popular today may be attributed to the fact that they are "good mixers" and uncommonly comfortable as an occasional chair.

Slender spindles, splayed legs, semi-circular seat and "stick" construction are the distinguishing marks of the Windsor chair. It originated in England and was popular in Charles Dickens' day, as can be seen from Seymour's illustrations of the Pickwick Papers in 1836. But a century before that, in 1730, a London advertisement reads: "All sorts of Windsor Garden chairs of all sizes, painted green or in the wood," proving, among other things, that the Windsor chair was already painted in colors in its earliest period. "Paint was a preservative and relieved austerity," according to *The Practical Book of American Antiques*, (Eberlein and McClure.)

In America we find further proof of this in James C. Tuttle's announcement in the *Salem Gazette*, August 19, 1796 of, "All kinds of Philadelphia Windsor Chairs and Settees... well painted with different colors, as the buyer chooses." Carl W. Dreppard, in his *Handbook of Antique Chairs*, quotes an existing bill, written by John Letchworth, Windsor chairmaker of Philadelphia, dated "1st day of month, 1796...18 oval-backed Windsor chairs painted white." Mr. Dreppard goes on to say, "Windsor chairs have been found in New England and Pennsylvania with but one coat of paint over the wood. The coat of paint is the color of black serge cloth—black with a tinge of green. Around the spindles there is evidence of decoration in the form of painted yellow rings. On a bill for chairs, issued by William Dutill of Philadelphia, dated May 1800, appear these entries: '4 dozen mahogany colored Windsor bow-back chairs. 8 dozen ditto, painted yellow and white. 9 settees painted green and yellow.' "

Philadelphia was the first place of record where American Windsors were made, hence they were often referred to as "Philadelphia Windsor Chairs," as in the James C. Tuttle advertisement. *(Fig. 42)*. But like all other types, the chair travelled. John Wadsworth advertises in the newspaper *American Mercury*, January 4, 1796, that he had come "to Hartford to carry on the Windsor chair making business."

Andrew Gautier, New York City's first Windsor chairmaker on record, advertised in the *New York Gazette*, April 18, 1765—"A large and neat assortment of Windsor Chairs. made in the best and neatest manner, and well painted." Gautier was probably the first man to illustrate his advertisements.

Another New York advertisement, that of a cabinet maker bidding directly for a shipper's trade, is that of Wheaton and Davis, which, for some months during 1819, appeared in the *Evening Post*. It reads, "Fancy and Mahogany Chairs and Sofa Manufactury. 156 Fulton Street opposite St. Paul's Church. Wheaton and Davis respectfully inform the public that they have for sale a large and elegant assortment of mahogany, curled maple, rosewood and fancy painted chairs, sofas, etc. richly ornamented in gold and bronze with hair, cane and rush seats. Shippers orders for any part of the continent executed with dispatch."

An advertisement of Nolan and Gridley, auctioneers, in the *Boston Columbian Centinel*, February 16, 1811, reads, "Nolan and Gridley have for sale at their ware room, Nos. 27 and 28 Cornhill—3,000 Chairs, comprising a very complete assortment, from the best workmanship and finest touch of the pencil to the most common, from 7 to 6 dlls. per doz. all which they will pack in shipping order and in the most careful manner."

The construction of a chair is our best guide to guessing its age. The earliest Windsors (early 18th century) were, for the most part, of the low-back style. Then came the comb-back, fan-back, and bow-back construction, with and without arms. And it was at the beginning of the 19th century when the Sheraton influence began to make itself felt on the Windsor chair with the rod-back, square top, bamboo turnings, stretchers at front and back, instead of one through the center.

We should bear in mind that the chair-maker filled commissions for sets of chairs made to order to suit the fancy of the buyer. Around 1800 and later there was a vogue in this country for the highly decorated, eye-catching Sheraton *fancy chair*, and it was very natural that it should affect the American Windsor. But if the Windsor was to keep pace with the fancy chair, a larger area to decorate than the simple Windsor afforded had to be created. The broader top slat, the step-down slat and arrow splats or spindles, and many other variations, not necessarily as pleasing

in proportion may have been developed for this purpose.

The Windsor chair seems to have had no special type of decoration. Sometimes designs were put on with a few painted brush strokes, similar to so-called "country painting," then again we find the more elegant freehand bronze technique used. We come across some that were stencilled with large, crude, single motifs, others with more complex, built-up designs. It seems that each decorator had his own ideas and used a free hand.

A great deal of research has been done on chairs but comparatively little on their ornamentation, and we find a good reason for this in the research material of Esther Stevens Brazer. She writes, "With all the wealth of decorated antiques that have survived the accidents of time, few are the names of those who are known to have done any of the ornamental work. Cabinet makers of distinction occasionally labelled some of their handiwork, but the decorators seem to have been a modest lot, keeping their identity very much in the background." However, thanks to Mr. N. Grier Parke of Woodstock, Vermont, we have learned quite a lot about a Windsor chairmaker and decorator named John White.

He was born in 1803 in the state of Vermont, on Happy Valley Creek, between Taftsville and Hartford. His father, Francis White, had been operating a chair shop since 1790, the remains of which are still standing. John's mother was Annis Tuttle of the Rutland publishing house family.

Mr. Parke, after a lifetime of being a mining engineer, has become a very fine chairmaker in his retirement, and a very discriminating collector of John White chairs. According to him, White opened his own chair shop in Woodstock in 1838, and nearly every old home in Windsor county contains one of his chairs. But they can also be found far from the Vermont hills where he lived. The Society for the Preservation of New England Antiquities in Boston owns one, and Mr. Parke tells me he once picked up a set of five side chairs in that city which bear every indication of John White construction. These were originally painted "dirty white" or, perhaps, a very light colonial yellow. There were three John White chairs in the Wadsworth Longfellow home in Portland, Maine, which has since been torn down. To Mr. Parke's distress no one knows what has become of the valuable chairs.

In his home state of Vermont, you will find sixteen John White settees in the Woodstock Town Hall, twenty-two more in the court house, and a wonderful sight they are. Their leg construction was used solely by John White. It is as if the long bench seat (8 foot 3) had been fastened to the legs of three separate chairs—one at each end, one in the middle. The effect is graceful, secure and unusual. The settees have plain top slats but all of them have the spindles installed fanning out slightly from the center, another characteristic feature of John White construction. The original bill of sale for these settees ($5 apiece) paid for half by the town, half by the county, is still on file. Mr. Parke found a John White bench that is 11½ feet long in Royalton, Vermont, Town Hall, but this one does not have the legs constructed at chair width.

Mr. Parke corroborated the fact that most Windsor chairs were painted. He says he has discovered traces of color on every Windsor

chair he has ever seen. Of his favorite chairmaker he says (in the *Decorator,* Vol. VI, Publication of the Historical Society of Early American Decoration, Inc.):

"In our family John White has been a tradition. . . . As a chairmaker he developed a distinctive type, based on Windsor forms, and each set. . .was made to order. . . . Except where sets are to be found, no two slats are identical—no spindles have just the same bend—no posts have the same swing—no seats the same measurement. . . . He also made benches of great delicacy, straight armchairs with and without comb-backs, Rockers with and without arms, Child's high-chairs, so-called Youth chairs, straight and with rockers, and Slipper chairs. . . . All of his chairs were not Stepdowns. The Comb-back Rocker at the Historical Society in Woodstock is unquestionably his work.

"Some of the peculiarities of his work might be of interest: The legs and rungs are all of the bamboo type and the striping is white, sometimes shaded with ocher, and he uses a great deal of white in his patterns. . . . The seats in his Comb-back chairs are as much as 19½" in depth and of varying widths, from 15" to 19". The arms are long and slender, of cherry, and the arm supports cut back sharply to accommodate the full skirts of the day, no doubt."

A long, wavy brush stroke was characteristic of John White's chair painting. He seemed fond of the shell motif and used sweeping grasses to fill in spaces. Although his designs were few and he used variations of them over and over again, they were always original, well balanced and attractive. Careful tracing of his patterns reveals that he used a stencil as a guide for painting the slats, arrow splats, stiles, seat fronts and, in some cases, even the outside of the rocker. His use of many background colors for chairs, from white to pink to near black, was unusual and effective. The color he used most frequently seems to have been a peculiar brown, very difficult to match, of which Mr. Parke always speaks as "John White brown."

In Esther Stevens Brazer's research material we find the name of a chair decorator which seems to have fascinated her just as much as his work, and no wonder! The man's name was Zophar Brooks (1812–1906) and he came of a family that did not go in for ordinary names. Other members were Sevi, Zenophon and Maro.

Zophar Brooks was born in Hancock, N.H. in 1812. He lived there to be 94 years old. Legend has it that he was six feet tall, straight as an arrow, with dark hair and very high color. In his youth he gilded the spire of a Hancock church. When he was eighty, realizing that the spire needed regilding and that he was the only gilder available, he once more climbed the tower and did the job over, all by himself.

Brooks did not make chairs. He bought them "in the white" and decorated them. Some stencils that he used to ornament chairs have been found, his stencils and gilding tools still exist, so do some of his striping brushes. Fig. 50 in Florence Wright's chapter on the Golden Age of Stencilling shows Zophar Brooks's stencilling kit. A Boston rocker, an armchair and a set of Hitchcock type chairs which he decorated are still in family possession. We show the armchair in Fig. 28.

In Esther Stevens Brazer's unpublished research material is a sketch of a very elegant chair with bamboo legs, painted sand color, with ornate striping and shaded gold leaf scroll on the top slat. This chair was marked "T. Wilder—Warranted" on the bottom and it was made in "Wilder Village," New Ipswich, N.H. by Peter Wilder and Sons between the years of 1802–1830. Their handcraft has been described in the town history. "T" was evidently one of Peter Wilder's sons.

Documented pieces such as these make us realize how important it is to be constantly alert for any identifying marks on original pieces. Perhaps you have a signed chair or one that has some historical data, and don't know it. Have you ever examined your old chairs carefully? Recently we turned over one and found written on the bottom: "Bought by Dolly Snell Noyes in 1822." *(Fig. 39).* A known decorator with originality, history and surviving examples of his work is so rare it is well worth searching for a trace of him in your antique furniture, going after more data and recording what you find.

The Sheraton influence on the Windsor chair shows in other ways than in its ornamentation. Suddenly the bulbous Windsor leg is gone. In its place we find the bamboo turned leg. In Fig. 3 the Sheraton influence is very evident in the construction of the back. The single center rung of early Windsors *(see Figs. 1, 2, 3, 4)* becomes, thanks to the Sheraton influence, two rungs on the outside, one front, one back. "Whenever the rungs are on the outside, we have lost real Windsor character," writes Wallace Nutting in his *Furniture Treasury,* under his illustration of the chair we show in Fig. 41. But all Windsors, early, late, and Sheraton influenced, show the "stick" construction, by which is meant that the spindles and the legs are "stuck" into the seat, a fraction of an inch from the edge. They are not a continuation of the back as in the Sheraton chair.

The ornamented Windsor chair is an outgrowth of the earlier pure forms of Sheraton and Windsor chairs and it is not easily typed as either one or the other. An effort has been made here to give distinguishing marks which may help you to identify them.

FIG. 1. *The bow-back or hoop-back Windsor chair.
1750–1800.
Courtesy of the Philadelphia Museum of Art.*

FIG. 2. *New England type. One piece bow-back Windsor
chair, with the hoop of the back forming the arms.
Well proportioned turnings and shaped feet.
Courtesy Miss Fanny Benedict, Warwick, New York*

FIG. 3. *Rod-back Windsor chair. 1800–25. Bamboo
turnings and straight lines of the back are characteristic of the Sheraton influence.
Courtesy Mr. & Mrs. Victor Starzinski, Burnt Hills,
New York.*

FIG. 4. *Fan-back side chair. 1750–1800. Desirable
Windsor features are the saddle-shape seat, the well-
proportioned turnings and the use of nine spindles
instead of the usual seven.
Courtesy Mr. Arthur Fellows, Lowville, New York*

FIG. 5. *Two John White chairs, photographed by Mr. Parke at Longfellow Home (now demolished) in Portland, Maine. Courtesy Mr. N. Grier Parke*

FIG. 5a. *Painted design on John White step-down Windsor, shown in Fig. 5. Note broad white striping.*

FIG. 5b. *A favorite painted design of John White, mainly white with vermilion overstrokes. Detail of chair in Fig. 5.*

FIG. 6. *Fan-back side-chair, similar to Fig. 4. Painted decoration. Called the "Westbrook Windsor." 1790–1805. Background dark red-brown.*
Former owner: Mr. Moreau L. Stoddard, Fairfield, Conn. Courtesy of Yale University Art Gallery.

FIG. 7. *Forerunner of the John White Windsor chair, probably made by his father, Francis White. Yellow striping on black is its only ornamentation. Authentic restoration by N. Grier Parke, Woodstock, Vermont. Courtesy Mr. Parke.*

FIG. 8. *Bench made by John White. Step-down slat. Design painted with white. Thin shading in red, yellow ochre and green. Striping all white.*
Courtesy Mr. N. Grier Parke

FIG. 8a. *Detail of John White bench in Fig. 8.*

FIG. 9 & 10. *Pair of white New York State Windsor chairs. Painted decoration, green sprays and accents. Courtesy of Mrs. Gordon Cole, Nicholsville, N. Y.*

FIG. 11. *Windsor bench, painted with running leaf ornamentation. Early 19th century. Courtesy of the Metropolitan Museum of Art. Gift of Mrs. Paul Moore, 1953.*

FIG. 12. *Detail of stencilled slat on one of six chairs, bought directly from John White and owned by the Williams family for three generations.*
Courtesy of Olive Williams Parke

FIG. 13a. Detail of Fig. 13.

FIG. 13. *Identified as a John White yoke-slat Windsor. Red-brown background, design yellowish white. Good illustration of the graceful lines of the Windsor chair with Sheraton influenced legs.*
Courtesy, Society for the Preservation of New England Antiquities

FIG. 14. *John White step-down Windsor, painted salmon pink. Brushstroke design, white and very dark green.*
Courtesy of Mr. N. Grier Parke

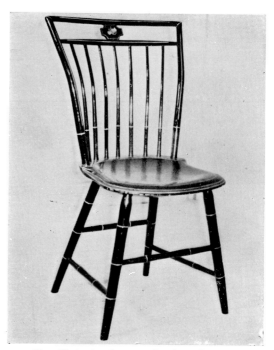

FIG. 15. *Made in the period when chairs in late Sheraton style were in vogue. 1800–25. The straight line type of back is the conspicuous feature. When a chair has as much Sheraton influence as this one, it* **might well be called a Sheraton-Windsor chair.** *Collection of Mrs. Arthur J. Oldham*

FIG. 16. *1800–25. Here step-down slat, spindles, seat and splayed legs are in the Windsor style, which is more dominant than the Sheraton influence, evident in the bamboo turnings.*
From the Oldham collection

FIG. 17. *Yellow Windsor side chair. 1800–15. Decorated with green brushstrokes and striping.*
Oldham collection

FIG. 18. *Sheraton influenced Windsor comb-back rocking chair. Dated on bottom, 1812. Painted decoration.*
Present owner unknown

FIG. 19. *"Stepped" comb-back rocking chair. c. 1800. Yellow chair with natural wood arms. Fine freehand bronze designs on back slat.*
Present owner unknown

FIG. 20. *Similar type, with freehand bronze decoration on top slat. Note fine, painted leaf-motifs on the front of the seat and on horizontal rails of back.*
Present owner unknown

FIG. 21. *Comb-back, step-down Windsor rocking chair. Ivory-white background. White roses, accented with vermilion, green and brown leaf sprays. John White type design.*
Present owner unknown

FIG. 22. *A splendid example of a comb-back Windsor chair with Sheraton influence. Note the continuous spindles supporting the comb, and the long, knife-blade rockers. c. 1820. Present owner unknown*

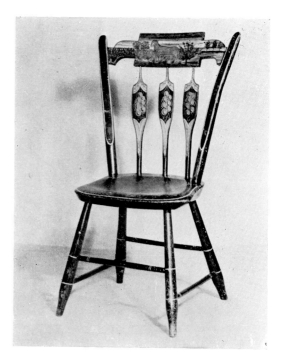

FIG. 23. *Windsor side chair, one of a pair originally from Rhode Island. Dark brown background. Biblical scene on top slat. Mid 19th Century. Strong Pennsylvania German influence in the decoration. Chair now in Farmer's Museum, Cooperstown, New York*

FIG. 24. *Windsor armchair, arrow slats. Gold leaf decoration on top slat and middle arrow. Gold leaf bands on legs. Otherwise yellow brush strokes and striping on mottled brown background. Courtesy Esther Oldham, Wellesley Hills, Mass.*

FIG. 25. *Windsor chair from farmhouse near Limerick, Maine. Probably yellow background with interesting putty-grained seat. Painted ornamentation, shells and acorns. Courtesy of Mrs. Wallace Bullard, Alfred, Maine*

FIG. 26. *Yellow Windsor armchair. Red cherry, natural wood arms. Painted decoration, authentically restored by E. S. Brazer.*
From the Oldham Collection

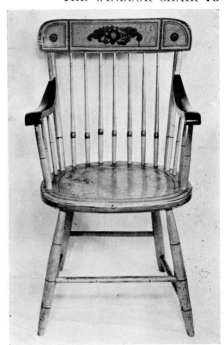

FIG. 27. *Common yellow armchair of the 1830's. Arms are left in natural mahogany. Putty-grained seat, freehand bronze decoration.*
Present Owner Unknown

FIG. 28. *Stencilled Windsor armchair, decorated by Zophar Brooks (1812–1906) Hancock, N.H., Made by F.C. Kittredge, Henneker, N.H.*
Present owner unknown

FIG. 29. *Common yellow chair, c. 1830. Freehand bronze decoration, gold leaf turnings or spindles, fancy brown grained seat.*
Owner: Bernice Drury, Springfield, Vermont

FIG. 30. *Painted arrow-back Windsor. c. 1810. Present owner unknown*

FIG. 31. *Windsor painted side chair. Present Owner Unknown*

FIG. 32. *Windsor side chair supposed to have been decorated by Henry Hartman, c. 1830, near Hopewell, N.J. Smoked background. Present owner unknown*

FIG. 33. *Painted arrow-back Windsor. Courtesy Florence E. Wright.*

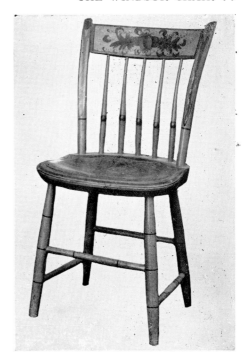

FIGS. 34 & 35. *Two yellow painted Windsors, c. 1830. Freehand bronze decoration with green brushstrokes. Gold turnings on spindles. Wide stripes transparent brown.*
Present owner unknown

FIG. 36. *Same type as Figs. 34 & 35. Background yellow. Freehand bronze decoration with black, painted scrolls. Transparent brown wide stripes. Gold turnings on back spindles. c. 1830.*
Owner Florence E. Wright

FIG. 37. *Same type yellow chair. Freehand bronze decoration.*
From the Oldham Collection

FIG. 38. *Unusual Sheraton type Windsor chair. Once owned by General Knox, Thomaston, Maine. c. 1840. Present owner unknown*

FIGS. 39 & 39a. *Fine example of Sheraton influenced Windsor chair painted straw color. Striped in thin brown and black. Black shadow outlines on freehand bronze decoration. Restrained use of gold lends elegance. Written on bottom seat: "Bought by Dolly Snell Noyes in 1822."*
Courtesy of Esther Oldham, Wellesley Hills, Massachusetts

FIGS. 40 & 40a. *Unusual Windsor swivel chair. Paper label grained background. Stencilled top slat. Arms painted with Owner: Mrs. Esther T. Broughton, Pleasant Point, Maine* *on bottom of seat says, "N. S. Denmark, Canton, Pa." Black a transparent brown paint (like varnish). Striping yellow.*

FIG. 41. *A late decorated Windsor. Sheraton influence. Courtesy Mrs. J. Stogdell Stokes, Bryn Mawr, Pa.*

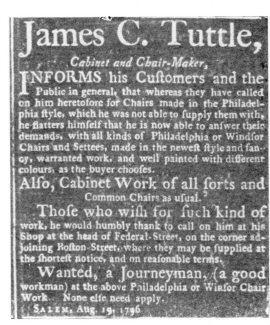

FIG. 42. *Appeared in the Salem Gazette, August 19 and 23, 1796.*
Still advertised as late as 1801.

CHAPTER IV

PLATE 4. *Crown-top, button-back. Legs straight and tapered at base. Signed:* "*L. Hitchcock, Hitchcocksville, Conn.*"
Owned by the Historical Society of Early American Decoration. Now at Farmer's Museum, Cooperstown, New York

THE EMPIRE PERIOD PRODUCES THE GOLDEN AGE OF STENCILLING

FLORENCE E. WRIGHT

TENCILLING with bronze powders produced an art that flourished for many years in the 1800's. It was an outgrowth of the fashionable styles of previous years. The elaborate imported lacquered furniture of the Orient was covered with raised gold motifs; the French used carved and gilded designs lavishly, much of the Louis XVI furniture was decorated with borders of brass or copper *ormulu* mounts that had been pressed into a raised, third-dimensional effect, with highlights and shadows.

At first gold leaf, with carefully etched details was used to resemble the raised gold and brass patterns, but it was natural that, with the growing popularity of gold decoration on furniture, an easier and less expensive method had to be found to obtain the same effect. Stencilling seemed to fit this need better than any other method of ornamentation.

The technique of stencilling, briefly, is that of polishing dry, finely ground bronze powders into a tacky varnish through the holes of a stencil. The first stencils were made of copy book paper but those used today are of architect's fine linen tracing cloth. Stencilled chairs of the best period had certain units stencilled with gold leaf. The leaf was placed over the stencil, then pushed down through it with a piece of plush, not velvet. Sometimes the ornament on the main slat contained a single unit which was made important by the use of gold or metal leaf. Twin cornucopias, for instance, were often treated in this way. The etching tool or fine brush was then used for outlining and shading on such motifs. *(Figs. 10, 11 and 12).*

Although the first stencilling was done on dark, rich woods such as mahogany or rosewood—especially pianos, wardrobes, tables, bureaus, mirrors—we find that on chairs it was used most often to adorn a grained effect that had been created by painting the common wood to resemble a rarer and more expensive type. Early chairs were often brown, with the graining pattern put on first with black, then covered with a brown varnish. Through the years, the most common background treatment was the black-over-red grained effect obtained by wiping some type of graining tool through a thin coat of black paint over a coat of Venetian red. (For more data on graining, see Chapter V.) Occasionally one finds a dark green or yellow chair, but the slat to be ornamented is usually black, to set off the bronze powders of the pattern through contrast. *(Fig. 61).*

The stencilled chair era of America comes up with a few famous names. The one we see most frequently is Lambert Hitchcock, who undoubtedly originated the type of chair that bears his name. He was a native of Cheshire, Conn., who settled in Barkhamsted, Conn. and established a cabinet and chair factory there in 1818. The settlement that sprang up around it became known as "Hitchcocksville."

At first he made only chair parts which he sold in large quantities, shipping them as far as Charleston, S.C. and other southern points. In 1825, however, he started producing finished chairs and was soon making as many as 15,000 a year, or 50 a day. He made a variety of styles, so that there was one to appeal to nearly everybody: Boston rockers and rocking settees, high slat-back and arrow-splat chairs, as well as many variations of the straight and arm chair. His chairs had rush, cane and, the later ones, plank seats. The frames were generally of birch or maple. One of the rarest types of early Hitchcock chairs is the high slat-back rocking chair shown in Chapter V, Fig. 1.

With what one might call 20th century business methods, Lambert Hitchcock advertised his chairs, not only in the papers but with his label: *L. Hitchcock, Hitchcocksville, Conn. Warranted, (Fig. 30b)* which was stencilled on the back of every seat frame. His brother-in-law, Arba Alford Jr., was Lambert Hitchcock's production manager and looked after the shop while Lambert traveled on business throughout New England and as far west and south as Chicago, St. Louis, and Philadelphia. In 1829, Lambert took his brother-in-law into the firm as a partner. Now the label read: *Hitchcock and Alford Co.*

In 1840 Lambert Hitchcock left Barkhamsted and settled in Unionville, Conn. where he opened a chair factory of his own again, signing his chairs *Lambert Hitchcock, Unionville, Conn.* Alford meanwhile took his brother into the business and went on making Hitchcock chairs which were labelled *Alford & Co.*

Lambert Hitchcock died in 1852. In 1866 the name of the settlement called "Hitchcocksville" was changed to Riverton, and in 1949, due to the revival of interest in stencilled furniture, the Hitchcock factory in Riverton was reopened and is now reproducing many of the old Hitchcock pieces. The patterns are the same, but today an airbrush is used in place of the velvet-covered finger with which stencilling was done over a hundred years ago.

According to a bill made out in "Hitchcocksville, 9th Oct. 1829...Mr. Pettibone Bo't of Lambert Hitchcock Assinees...9 cane seat chairs @ $1.50...$13.50. ... Rec'd payment for my assinees...Lambert Hitchcock." Today Hitchcock chairs retail at from $40 to $45, and a $39.50 stencilled Boston rocker was shown at the American exhibition in Moscow in 1959 as a "typical" piece of furniture to be found in the American home.

The Hitchcock chair is nearly always ornamented and it is usually stencilled. Sometimes it is referred to as an "American Empire chair." The broad back slats afford excellent space for ornamentation. See Fig. 37 for a typical Hitchcock pattern that you can find used over and over again by different decorators. It has been called the "most used and abused chair pattern."

With his name and address stamped on the back of each chair, it was only natural for the term "Hitchcock chair" to become generally used for the type resembling those he made. Over fifty factories made Hitchcock type chairs but very few labelled them. Some exceptions we have come across are: Churchill and Co., Wm. Moore Jr., Holmes and Roberts. The ornamentors, however, seem to have remained obscure. This may have been because it was the women and children employed by Lambert Hitchcock who ornamented the chairs. The children applied the first coat of paint, the women did the decorating, and these early patterns formed the basis for all future decoration of Hitchcock type chairs. The illustrations for this chapter give a fairly comprehensive picture of many of the more popular examples.

One of the few early stencillers whose name has been preserved for us was Thomas Jefferson Gildersleeve (1805–1871), *gilder and maker of Furniture and Chairs of all descriptions,* according to the trade card of his New

York shop. As a boy of fifteen he was apprenticed to Richard Tweed, chairmaker of New York City, and lived with the family until 1827, when he was old enough to open his own shop at 237–239 Delancey Street, at the back of his house, above his stables. Here he worked with two apprentices until the house had to be razed to build the Delancey Street bridge. He moved to 197 Chatham Street where he went into business with another early craftsman called Madden. Gildersleeve retired in 1861 and died ten years later, at the age of sixty-six. (See Fig. 29 for an authentic Gildersleeve chair.)

Forty authentic Gildersleeve stencils have been found, typical of patterns used on chairs from the 1820's on. They show fruit, flowers and leaves cut in one stencil, pomegranates with stems attached, a single-unit rose, and are indications of the simplification of the art of stencilling as it became increasingly popular and in ever greater demand.

A famous "upstate New York" furniture maker and stenciller was Ransom Cook (1794–1854) who opened a shop in Saratoga Springs as a young man of nineteen. His business prospered so that in 1827–28 he erected a new home and factory on South Broadway. Ransom Cook made many fine stencil patterns for chairs, some of which are shown in Figs. 34, a–d. These patterns were photographed by Esther Stevens Brazer through the courtesy of Mr. Clarence W. Mosher of Ballston Spa. Mr. Mosher had found, in an antique shop, an account book of Ransom Cook's which contained the old stencils in its pages—the years included were from 1823 to 1834—and Mr. Mosher used these stencils in his work as a decorator for a number of years. At his death in 1958, they were given to the Saratoga His-

torical Society, where they can be seen today.

William Eaton (1819–1904) of Boston, called "the best stenciller in New England," gave us the finest stencilling and designing of the late-middle and late periods. He was one of three brothers, all of whom were noted for their fine work. Eaton made many of his own designs and, according to a colleague, George Lord, "no pattern was too intricate for his knife."

He was born in Salem, Mass. but did most of his work in Boston. He had a shop in Fulton Street in 1845, later he worked in various shops, carrying on his work sporadically. Of Eaton's work, Janet Waring writes, "He learned how to build with single units, to shade and secure perspective, to apply veins both with the curved paper and with the separate stencils, and to follow the quicker method of making a complex design with as few as one or two cut-outs, for during his working years he had to compete with those who made chair slats in a single pattern and applied their gold without shading."

A portfolio of Eaton stencils was discovered by Janet Waring and many of them are illustrated in her book, *Early American Stencils*. Eaton first learned how to do the early shaded work, then he developed all later types. He was especially skillful in the use of color washes over the stencil and the freehand painting of flowers used on the Victorian type of furniture, which he combined with a stencilled framework. Sometimes he signed his chairs, working his signature, *W. P. Eaton*, into the stencilled pattern. We find this quite often in the corner of the top slat of his Boston rockers. It helps us to identify other chairs, unsigned, as quite probably his. In Chapter V on the Rocking Chair, Fig. 50 shows a chair with Eaton type decoration. See also Fig. 29, with detail, in Chapter VI.

Stencilled chairs of a characteristic type are found in the Rochester, New York, area, with the label of Charles Robinson stamped on the back of the top slat. They are of the 1850 and 1860 period and are either Boston rockers or the simple two-slat chairs with unturned posts and legs. (See Chapter V, Figs. 42, 43 and 44.)

Robinson came to Rochester from Connecticut with his brothers when the Erie Canal was opened in 1825, and he made chairs and other furniture for many years. His mass production of chairs was aided in 1858 by being associated with the Western House of Refuge, later the State Agricultural and Industrial School in Industry, N.Y. By contract, Robinson provided the tools and machines and the school furnished the boys who made the cane and flag seats.

Jarred Johnson (1801–1873) was another well-known stenciller of his day. He worked in Sheffield, Mass., just over the Connecticut border. He was recognized for his beautifully shaded composite patterns and his fine borders. Many exact geometric figures were incorporated in his patterns. He was possibly one of the first craftsmen to decorate Hitchcock chairs.

After going out of style when the carved rosewood, mahogany and walnut furniture became the fashion, stencilling gradually became a "lost art." Interest in it was revived in this century through the dedicated research of Janet Waring and through the writings and teachings and research of Esther Stevens Brazer and her students. We are indebted to them for the appreciation and preservation of many fine originals in homes and museums,

and for photographs and records of patterns used by early artists, as for instance, George Lord.

George Lord (1833–1928) of Portland, Maine, was the last of the old-time decorators. He started decorating chairs in 1848, serving his apprenticeship under Frances Holland, who had previously worked in Halifax, Canada, and Boston. He was a meticulous craftsman and in 1925, at the age of ninety-two, was still working with a clear eye and a steady hand. He could stripe as well with his left hand as with his right and could load his square-tipped brush with three shades of pink paint and, with a deft twist of his wrist, paint a rose. He was an expert on so-called rosewood graining and in his lifetime of work learned to master all the techniques involved in Hitchcock type and Victorian chair ornamentation. He died at the age of ninety-five.

Mr. Lord's experience as a decorator and striper was passed on to both Mrs. Brazer and Janet Waring, who knew him personally. When they became interested in learning the lost art of furniture stencilling, he generously taught them what he knew about the early techniques. We have this start that he gave them to thank for the knowledge passed on to us by these two women, who are responsible for the present widespread interest in a fascinating and practical art.

Today many chairs are being restored by enthusiastic hobbyists who like to refinish and decorate furniture. From attic and barns and all around the house, chairs that have been stored away or covered with many layers of paint are being restored and redecorated. Craftsmen are interested in studying the changes in stencilling techniques as they developed from the earliest works of about

1817, through the best years of 1825–1835, into the declining years which lasted until about 1870. They follow the usual pattern of any art development: first—intricate fine detail and workmanship of individual pieces by expert craftsmen, then the details becoming gradually coarser, the methods simpler as quantity production becomes an important factor and, finally, in later pieces, crude, simple techniques and workmanship.

The early work is far more beautiful. Early stencil patterns, dating back to 1817–25, are delicate and exquisitely shaded to bring out highlights where they belong and give the design a lifelike reality. The stencil is perfectly cut and the design meticulously composed— bowl or basket containing flowers or fruit, cornucopia, shell, rose or symbols, such as lyre and eagle. Anyone who has ever stencilled knows what this means, how much more difficult it is, for instance, to *model* the veins of a leaf with an arc of linen than to superimpose veins already cut. Between 1825–30, presumably to gain the speed required by more rapid production demands, a new method was adopted, which Esther Stevens Brazer liked to call the "hit-or-miss" method. A focal point was chosen as the center of the pattern and less important motifs were set around it until the space was filled. All details were coarser, therefore more easily cut and the cutting itself was less perfect. We find the same motif repeated over and over again. "It is quicker to reapply the stencil in your hand than to lay it down and select a different one," Mrs. Brazer writes in her notes. By 1835, many stencil patterns were being cut and applied in one piece. They were large and crude. Yet in restoring furniture of this period, only a pattern of the same age as the chair is appropriate and looks right on it.

In examining fine originals or their photographs, one is impressed with the importance of being authentic in one's restorations and realizes that the details of chair shapes indicate the need for certain types of patterns, the use of certain colors and techniques. Only by careful study and by following these coordinated details can we be justified in our work. Especially is this true of those who make restorations for others and many are seeing this absorbing hobby develop into a quite profitable business.

A brief outline of the characteristics of the different periods of stencilling follows:

A GUIDE FOR THE STUDY OF STENCILLED CHAIRS

Early Characteristics

CHAIR SHAPES   Fine proportions and graceful curves. Legs often splay outward.

HAND-GRIP   Pillow shape the most common. Some roll tops.

MAIN SLAT   Decorative shapes such as cutout, cornucopias and eagle. Designs include fruit and leaves.

BACKGROUND   Brown, with artificial graining.

ORNAMENTATION   Gold leaf used on handgrips and stiles, front of seats and most of pattern. Wide use of gold stripes.

STRIPES   Go all around posts.

DETAILS OF PATTERNS   Intricate and carefully executed.

VEINS   Shaded with powders against a curved edge of stencil.

STENCILS   Cut with separate units for each part of design.

POWDERS Gold and silver powders used, skillfully blended and polished for brilliance.

Intermediate Period Characteristics

BACKGROUND Black-over-red, grained.

HANDGRIPS Pillow and roll shapes.

MAIN SLAT Plain, turtle and button styles.

ORNAMENTATION All patterns stencilled. Fruit and flower designs, landscapes. Details larger and less intricate.

STRIPES Drawn only part way around posts so as to be seen only from front.

STENCILS Cut as separate units and assembled until around 1830, then some parts, such as leaves and stems, were cut in one stencil.

VEINS Stencilled.

POWDERS Colored powders such as copper and red were added to the pallet. Colors were skillfully blended from one to the other, red was used for flower centers.

PAINT About 1830, transparent oil colors were used on some patterns over the stencilled flowers or fruit. Black and green opaque color was used for scrolls and leaves on some patterns.

Late Characteristics

CHAIR SHAPES Less refined shapes and turnings. Fiddle or banister backs around 1840. Victorian about 1845. Simple turned chair about 1850 and 1860.

BACKGROUND Black-over-red. Some yellow.

ORNAMENTATION Stencilled patterns, often with colored over-tones. Landscapes. Flowers painted freehand.

STRIPES Coarse striping in yellow paint on the very late ones. Gold not used except on the early ones of this period. Some green stripes.

STENCILS Each area cut in one stencil.

POWDERS Gold, silver and orange, polished with little or no shading. Very little shading of one part to another.

PAINT Continued use of oil colors for realistic designs, transparent oil colors used as a wash over bronze powders for late one-stencil designs.

FIG. 1. *Directoire carved and gilded mahogany chair, attributed to Duncan Phyfe. 1815. The carved cornucopia later developed into a flat slat with stencilled cornucopias.*
Courtesy Ginsburg & Levy, Inc., Madison Ave., New York City.

FIG. 2. *Carved and gilded Directoire chairs. Present owner unknown*

FIG. 3. *Directoire type, showing Sheraton influence.*
Owner unknown

FIG. 4. *Brown chair with Sheraton and Directoire characteristics.*
Courtesy Mrs. Appleton

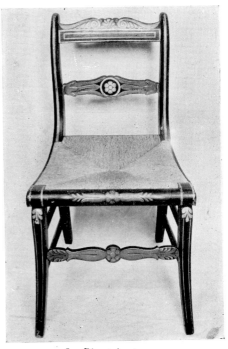

FIG. 5. *Directoire type.*
Courtesy Mrs. Gladys G. Brown

FIG. 6. *One of a set of six chairs, purchased in Seville, Spain.*
Courtesy Mrs. Madeline Wills, Black Horse Tea Room, Hingham, Mass.

FIG. 7. *Advertisement in the Hartford Courant, 1824.*

FIG. 8. *Cut-out slat with gold leaf scrolls, combined with stencilling.*
Mrs. Arthur Oldham Collection, Wellesley Hills, Mass.

FIG. 9. *Shaped slat with all-stencilled design. Gold leaf handgrip, top of stile and front of seat patterns, with stencilled stile pattern.*
Courtesy Miss Vivian Waters, Ithaca, New York

FIG. 10. *Early transition type. Stencilling combined with gold leaf.*
Courtesy Miss M. C. Appleby, near Providence, Rhode Island

FIG. 11. *c. 1825. Stencilling combined with gold leaf.*
Courtesy Mrs. Helen C. Edmunds

FIG. 12. *White chair with gold leaf and bronze decoration.*
Courtesy Mrs. W. H. Seward, Auburn, New York

FIG. 13. *This chair illustrates the transition from gold leaf to all-stencilled decoration. From 1830 to 1850.*
Courtesy Mrs. Oliver Wolcott

FIG. 13a. *Detail of Fig. 13.*

FIG. 14. *All designs on this chair are stencilled. Courtesy Mrs. Barbara K. Bird, Boonville, New York*

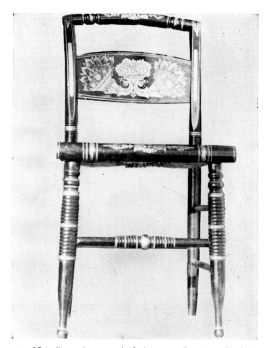

FIG. 15. *One of a set of chairs near Saratoga Springs. Probably a Ransom Cook. Owner unknown*

FIG. 16. *This chair, with many fine features, was in the collection of Esther Stevens Brazer. Ornamented by Ransom Cook.*

FIG. 17. *Curly maple chair. Stencilling with black, painted accents. Ornamented by Ransom Cook. Present owner unknown*

FIG. 18. *One of a set of six chairs, stencilled, Sheraton influence.*
Courtesy Stephen Van Rennselaer, Peterborough, New Hampshire

FIGS. 19 & 19a. *From a set of eagle-back plank-seated chairs.*
Courtesy Mrs. Philip H. Horton, Peconic, L. I., New York

FIG. 20a. *Detail of Fig. 20.*

FIG. 20. *Button-back yellow chair. Here the eagle is not carved out. The design is in gold leaf, green and black. Burnt sienna is used for shading the gold leaf. Courtesy Miss Anna Magner, Hingham, Mass.*

FIG. 21a. *Detail of Fig. 21.*

FIG. 21. *Early stencilled turtle-back. c. 1830. Note Directoire legs. Courtesy H. H. Ferris, Montclair, New Jersey*

FIG. 22. *Turtle-back, roll-top.*
Courtesy Mr. William Richmond,
Stamford, Connecticut

FIG. 22a. *Detail of Fig. 22.*

FIG. 23. *Turtle-back, which may be a Ransom Cook*
chair. c. 1825.
Courtesy Mrs. Roland Thaxter

FIG. 23a. *Detail of Fig. 23.*

FIG. 24. *Dark green chair with main slat painted black, to set off the stencilled work. Probably a Gildersleeve chair, as some of the units were found in his stencils.*
Courtesy Florence E. Wright

FIG. 25. *Dark green with main slat painted black, as in Fig. 24.*
Courtesy Mrs. C. E. Pearsall, Covert, New York

FIG. 26. *Crown-top with gold leaf design, button-back slat with stencilled pattern using the pineapple as the central motif. (The pineapple was the symbol of hospitality.)*
Owner unknown

FIG. 27. *Button-back roll-top.*
Courtesy Mrs. Philip Horton, Peconic, L. I., New York

FIG. 28. *Crown-top, button-back. Legs straight and tapered at base. Signed: "L. Hitchcock, Hitchcocksville, Conn." Owned by Hist. Soc. of Early American Decoration. Now at Farmer's Museum, Cooperstown, New York.*

FIG. 29. *A late Gildersleeve chair. Courtesy Mrs. J. H. Murray*

FIG. 30a. *Detail of Fig. 30.*

FIG. 30. *Hitchcock chair with early label: "L. Hitchcock, Hitchcocksville, Conn. Warranted."*
From the Collection of Mrs. Arthur Oldham, Wellesley Hills, Mass.

FIG. 30b. *Label on Fig. 30.*

FIG. 31. *Chair with similar pattern, labelled "Wm. Moore Jr." Shows heavy graining. Courtesy Mrs. Gilbert Jones*

FIG. 31a. *Detail of Fig. 31.*

FIG. 31b. *Label on Fig. 31.*

FIG. 32. *Present owner unknown.*

FIG. 32a. *Detail of Fig. 32.*

FIG. 33. *Courtesy of Florence E. Wright.*

FIGS. 34 & 34a. *These patterns from the Ransom Cook stencils were photographed by Esther Stevens Brazer through the courtesy of the late Mr. Clarence Mosher of Ballston Spa, New York, who found them in the old account book of Ransom Cook. They are now in the collection of the Saratoga Historical Society. They show typical types of patterns used in the 1820's and early 1830's.*

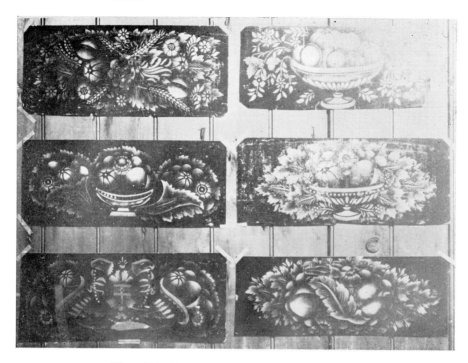

FIGS. 34b, c, & d. *More patterns from the Ransom Cook stencils.*

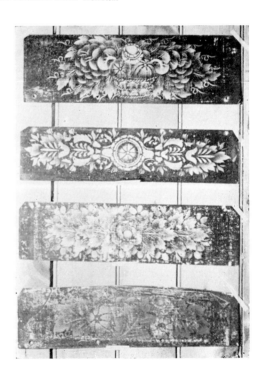

FIG. 35. *Crown-top slat. This chair has a
"Hitchcock and Alford" label.
Courtesy Mrs. Gordon Spencer*

FIG. 35a. *Detail of design in Fig. 35.*

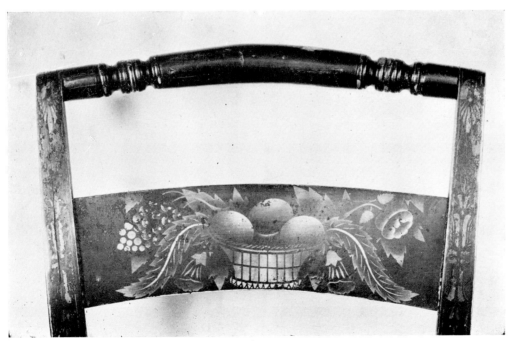

FIG. 36. *Detail of crown-top slat chair, with same pattern as in Fig. 35.
Courtesy Florence E. Wright*

FIG. 37. *The diamond-shaped slats usually have side borders. A favorite of Mrs. Brazer's. Used to teach her pupils how to shade grapes and the veins on leaves.*
Courtesy Mr. J. J. Shay

FIG. 37a. *Close-up of Fig. 37.*

FIG. 38. *This pattern is the same as shown in Fig. 34a, showing the designs of Ransom Cook.*
Courtesy Mrs. E. A. Norton, Cambridge, Massachusetts.

FIG. 38a. *Close-up of Fig. 38.*

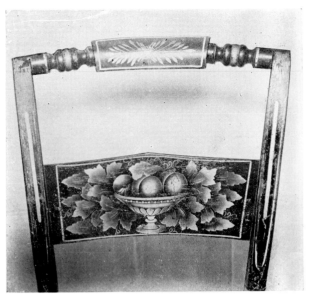

FIG. 39. *The bowl of fruit was a favorite pattern and had many variations.*
Courtesy Mrs. McGraw

FIG. 40. *The narrow slat, with intricately designed pattern and the small gold leaf designs are indications of an early chair.*
Courtesy Mrs. Gail H. Helmer, Chelsea, Vermont

FIG. 41. *Child's chair, showing the customary use of the same sized units as were used on chairs for adults.*
Courtesy Mrs. George Dalney, Medfield, Massachusetts

FIG. 42. *Unusual pattern, with some of the early gold leaf decoration on the hand grip and front of seat.*
Mrs. J. Lewis, Warren, Rhode Island

FIG. 43a. *Detail of Fig. 43.*

FIG. 43. *The lyre was used as the center motif on many chairs. The side units, cut in one stencil, indicate a design after 1830.*
Present owner unknown

FIG. 44. *Early two-slat chair with many characteristics of the Directoire period. Gold leaf acanthus leaves are used on the legs and stiles. Fine detail in slat patterns.*
Courtesy Mrs. Fred Guyle, Penn Yan, N.Y.

FIG. 45. *Landscapes were favorite subjects around 1840–45.*
Courtesy Mr. A. H. Rice, Bethlehem, Pa.

FIG. 46. *An early "late" chair of the 1850 and 1860 period. The stencils are cut in one piece and a red overtone is washed over the flowers.*
Courtesy Florence E. Wright

FIG. 47. *This chair has both slats with a symmetrical pattern. This is not usual, as most chairs have an informally placed center unit on the top slat.*
Courtesy Theophile J. Olbertz

FIG. 47a. *Close-up of Fig. 47.*

FIG. 48. *Two-slat, brown, grained chair. The top slat has a rolled edge.*
Courtesy Mrs. William J. Schwab, Gainesville, New York

FIG. 49. *Courtesy Mrs. C. E. Pearsall, Covert, New York.*

FIG. 50. *Stencil kit of Zophar Willard Brooks (see Chap. III), decorator and gilder of Hancock, N.H. These Stencils illustrate a late type, with as much cut in one stencil as could conveniently be used.*
Courtesy Mr. Maro S. Brooks, Hancock, New Hampshire

FIG. 51. *Plank-seat chair, having the label: "J. B. Hatch, Warranted."*
Courtesy Mr. Higgins, Wells, Maine

FIG. 52. *A series of late stencil designs. From 1830 to 1850.*

FIG. 53. *Courtesy Mrs. Gail H. Helmer, Chelsea, Vermont.*

FIG. 54. *A very handsome fiddle-back chair. Corners on top slat similar to Boston rockers. Fine cutting on top slat. Courtesy Ginsberg & Levi, Inc., Madison Ave., New York City*

FIG. 54a. *Detail of the fiddle-back chair, showing an interesting use of the maker's name as part of the design. "Made by M. L. Gates, Boston." Stencilled by William Eaton.*

FIG. 55. *A design of strawberries was used in the center of the top slat, and a bird on a bough on the urn-shaped center panel. Made by the Union Chair Co. Courtesy Mr. I. Johnson, Winsted, Conn.*

FIG. 55a. *Detail of Fig. 55 showing label.*

FIG. 56. *Stencils from the Cutting and Morrell factory, Albany, New York. These stencils are now in the Metropolitan Museum of Art, New York City.*

FIG. 57. *Another typical pattern for the fiddle-back chair. Landscapes, especially with boats, were used a great deal of the time. From the collection of Mrs. John Oldham, Wellesley Hills, Mass.*

FIG. 57a. *Close up of Fig. 57.*

FIG. 58a. *Detail of Fig. 58, showing label.*

FIG. 58. *Two-slat chair labelled "Holmes and Roberts, Colebrook, Conn. Warranted."*
Courtesy Mrs. Julius Whiting, Colebrook, Conn.

FIG. 59. *Late two-slat Windsor type, stencilled. c. 1838.*
Courtesy Florence E. Wright

FIG. 60. *Late version, two-slat stencilled chair, yellow-brown mottled seat. Top slat has transparent color washed over the stencil. About 1850.*
Courtesy Mrs. Richard Gordon

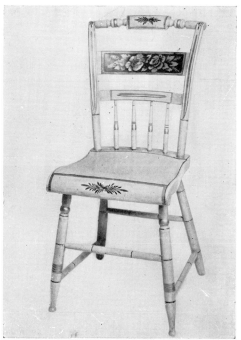

FIG. 61. *Yellow wooden-seat chair of the Hitchcock type, showing how the decorator made a black panel for his stencilling. About 1835.*
Present owner unknown

FIG. 62. *Two chairs having typical late patterns with a single stencil used, and the color added, for some of the flowers. Usually only red was used, with no coloring on the leaves.*
Courtesy of Florence E. Wright

FIG. 63. *"Chamber" or "Night" chair of the 1850's and 1860's.
This chair has a top slat similar to many Boston rockers found in
the counties around Rochester, New York. Probably a Robinson
piece.*
Owner unknown

FIG. 64. *One type of decoration used in the 1845–1860 years, with a wide gold band and landscapes with build-
ings and, often, people, dogs and horses.*
Courtesy Mrs. Charles Slaughter, Warwick, New York

PLATE 5. *Yellow rocker with natural wood arms. An early design combining gold leaf and freehand bronze.*
Courtesy of Mrs. Carl F. Gilbert, Ithaca, N.Y.

THE ROCKING CHAIR BRINGS COMFORT TO SIMPLE HOMES

HELEN WARREN CHIVERS

EAR THE TURN of the century, a close relative of ours lost his wife. He engaged a house-keeper from Maine, one of a family of eighteen children. Returning home from his office one evening, he asked her what she did with herself all day. She told him, "Sometimes I rock an' read, or I rock an' knit, an' then again I just set an' rock. . . ."

I remember the chair she rocked in very well. It was a Boston rocker. Its place was in the kitchen, by the south window, near the stove. It is comforting to realize that there is nothing unique about this recollection. Many of us, I am sure, can recall just such a kitchen, with its fixed location for a favorite rocking chair and they are probably as delighted as I am that the kitchen, as a family room, is coming into its own again in country homes, with a fireplace and a rocker by the hearth.

The origin of the rocking chair is shrouded in about as much doubt and controversy as the origin of Shakespeare's plays, but I am not going to be fanatic about claiming it for Benjamin Franklin. All I intend to do is pass on to you briefly the few facts we have to go by when we attribute this invention to him.

The diary of the Reverend Manasseh Cutler, who was prominent in the politics of Ohio in his time, tells us about a visit to Benjamin Franklin in Philadelphia on July 17th, 1787, as follows: "After it was dark, we went into the house and the Doctor invited me into his library which is likewise his study. . . . He showed us his long, artificial arm and hand, for taking down and putting books up on high shelves which are out of reach; and his great armed chair with rockers, and a large fan placed over it, with which he fans himself,

keeps off flies, etc. while he sits reading, with only a slight motion of his foot; and many other inventions *all his own*, but of lesser note." Thus a whole theory can have its beginnings on such thin evidence as the three words *all his own*, (the italics are mine) which might refer to the "armed chair with rockers" or only to the "many other inventions."

True, we have earlier evidence of the existence of the rocking chair in a handwritten bill of the famous Philadelphia furniture maker, William Savery. On February 11, 1774, thirteen years prior to the Reverend Cutler's visit to Benjamin Franklin, Mr. Savery charged Mrs. Mary Morris one shilling tenpence for "bottoming a rocking chair." From the fact that Mr. Savery had been asked to *re*seat a rocking chair in 1774, we can conclude that the chair was not new, and can grope our way back through the mists of research another ten, even twenty years, placing the date for the earliest rocking chairs somewhere about 1750, and still not rob Benjamin Franklin of any glory. He could very well have conceived the idea of putting rockers on a straight chair twenty-four years before the Reverend's visit which took place, after all, when Dr. Franklin was past eighty. And we are fairly safe in concluding that the rocking chair was an American innovation. Europe was not enthusiastic about them.

An amusing European viewpoint on the rocking chair is offered by Harriet Martineau, who writes in 1838, in her *Retrospect of Western Travel:* "In these small inns (between Stockbridge and Albany) the disagreeable practice of rocking in the chair is seen in its excess. In the inn parlors are three or four rocking chairs in which sit ladies who are vibrating in different directions and at various velocities, so as to try the head of a stranger. ... How this lazy and ungraceful indulgence ever became general, I cannot imagine; but the nation seems so wedded to it, that I see little chance of its being forsaken. When American ladies come to live in Europe, they sometimes send home for a rocking chair. A common wedding present is a rocking chair. A beloved pastor has every room in his house furnished with a rocking chair by his grateful and devoted people. ..."

The earliest type of rocking chair was a straight chair, converted by having rockers added. Early rockers were short and stubby and were probably inspired quite simply by the cradle. The high, cradle-shaped rocker, the thin, knife-blade rocker and the flat, thick rockers into which an altered leg was set, were shaped the same back and front and extended an equal distance. Only later was the back of the rocker extended until we find it outstretching the front by four, eight, sometimes as much as ten inches. This gave a more soothing rocking effect and more pleasing proportions, but it made the rocking chair a menace to your ankles and instep, according to those who won't have one in the house because they can't seem to keep out of its way!

There are people who assume that when a rocking chair has side-stretchers, it is a converted chair which, according to Mrs. Brazer is "stretching a point too far." Certainly those with no side rungs usually started out in life as rocking chairs. *(Fig. 3)*. But we find many later types with side rungs which were rocking chairs from the start. You may be fairly sure, though, that if the side rungs are disproportionately low *(Fig. 17)* or if the legs have been sawed off, the rocking chair has been converted.

We find several methods used in affixing rockers to a chair. Generally a socket is cut into the bottom of the chair leg and a thin, "knife-blade" rocker is set in perpendicularly. Sometimes we find the rocker attached to the outside of the legs. *(Fig. 9)*. A process usually found only in true rocking chairs was the lathe-turning of the chair leg to a point, which was set into a wide rocker. *(Fig. 15)*. But then again you may come across a chair which refutes all these fine theories because some chairmaker decided to put equidistant rockers on a straight chair fifty years after they had gone out of style, or some housewife wanted her rocker to be "just like grandma's." *(Fig. 16)*. This gives us a good example of the confusion of styles that make all conclusions as to date hazardous unless backed up by at least a chairmaker's name. The back of this chair, with its three narrow splats separated by small balls, is in the Sheraton style, although a little heavier, and the rest is Windsor. This chair was in the Andrews family home in Meriden, N. H. about 1852. It was always referred to as "the Sheraton Fancy."

As far as we know, rockers were first put on simple type chairs such as the slat-back, Windsor, and Pennsylvania German chairs. Later we find Hitchcock chairs converted into rockers and the Hitchcock factory was probably the first to manufacture rocking chairs as a *factory* product. Of course they made what was termed "true rockers," not conversions. They manufactured Boston rockers, both large and small, with and without arms and with the rolled seat; children's Boston rockers and the cradle settee, sometimes called the Cape Cod cradle rocker or Mammy rocker. *(Figs. 53 and 54)*. The latter was especially popular and practical.

We find ornamentation on many rocking chairs—the traditional stencils on Hitchcock rockers, Pennsylvania German designs on the rocking chairs coming from that region and appropriate designs on the late Windsor rockers. Early Windsor chairmakers seem to have been accustomed to painting and striping their chairs but not to decorating them ornately. However, when Sheraton Fancy ideas began to invade the Windsor chair shops, the chairmaker was forced to call in a decorator or finisher to ornament the chair for him if he was not capable of doing so himself. Not that I want to belittle the beauty and ornamental effect of painting and striping alone. Striping is one of the most important aspects of ornamentation. It accents the line of the chair's construction and is often used to form very intricate patterns of its own, down the stiles, along the arms or sides of the rockers (*Fig. 54*), and to frame the design on slat or seat. It could be narrow or wide, and varied in color with the background color of the chair. The earliest striping, in gold leaf or yellow paint, replaced the satinwood inlay of the Hepplewhite pieces and the brass inserted lines on English Sheraton pieces. Sheraton refers to "the good effect of black chairs finished with yellow lines which suggest the inlay known as stringing." Yellow, according to him, was "King's yellow, white and a trifle orange."

Fine graining could do for a chair just as much as intricate design, and a whole book could be written about it. We have space to mention only a few types. One popular method was called "vinegar graining." Dry umber powder was added to cider vinegar to make a thin paint. This was spread over a coat of yellow ocher. Then the decorator took a piece of putty, rolled it between his palms until he had a soft roll, about the size of his thumb, and pressed the end of this putty thumb around the edge of the seat in connecting blobs. Any pattern could be worked out in this way—semi-circles which joined, a hit-or-miss pattern, a shell pattern—until the seat was covered. For interesting seat graining see Fig. 32.

There were other types of graining done with corncobs, sponges, feathers, and other graining forms, all of which resulted in a variety of grained patterns. Tortoiseshell graining is done much the same way except that the thin black paint is rubbed off in "swirls." There is also a coarse graining done by putting the red paint *over* the black in slanting daubs. Many Hitchcock chairs show this type of graining. Florence Wright, in her chapter on the Golden Age of Stencilling, tells of the over-all graining effect imitating rosewood or walnut. The seats of Boston Rockers were very often grained. Fig. 39 is a particularly fine example, and the art of graining has been beautifully reproduced by Thelma Riga, a member of the Esther Stevens Brazer Guild, in the Boston Rocker she ornamented, which is shown in Chapter VII, Fig. 3.

Of the Boston Rocker, Wallace Nutting says, in his *Furniture Treasury*, "The most popular chair ever made, the type which people use, antiquarians despise and novices seek," which covers the subject very well. The Boston Rocker was an outgrowth of the Windsor chair. How it came by its name, we do not know. Most likely it was first manufactured in that city.

The top slat of the Boston Rocker was usually lavishly ornamented. Even the roll seat, designed most successfully for comfort, came in handy for ornamentation. Frequently only a conventional unit, framed with striping, was used on the front of the seat, but very often we find quite elaborate motifs matching a handsomely decorated top slat. Sometimes the Boston Rocker slat was decorated in freehand bronze and gold leaf, with painted brush strokes; more often than not, though, it was stencilled.

The Boston Rocker had various types of stencilled designs. A popular pattern for the top slat was a bowl, basket or cornucopia, filled with flowers, fruit, and leaves. English Staffordshire porcelain patterns and the Hudson River school of painting were making landscape scenes popular. It was natural that they should put in an appearance on furniture and the broad top slat of the Boston Rocker seems to have occurred to stencillers as an ideal place for them. Sometimes the scene depicted is in commemoration of an historic event. One is reminded of the stencilled tray commemorating the first English railroad that ran between Liverpool and Manchester in 1830, or the small clock glass that shows, in reverse painting, a balloon with two people in the basket and commemorates the first aeronaut who successfully accomplished the voyage across the Irish Channel from Dublin, Ireland, July 22, 1818.

We do not always know the stories connected with these patterns but feel sure that there is one to go with many of them. Quite clearly the design on the broad slat of Fig. 36 commemorates the *Savannah*, the first steam side-wheeler to cross the Atlantic, and the *William Henry Harrison Rocker (Fig. 38)* is decorated to immortalize his "Log Cabin and Hard Cider" campaign of 1840.

Anybody who has done thorough research

on the Boston Rocker has probably learned to tell dates by the design at the curved ends of the top slat. . .as well as you can hope to tell dates in the research of a craft that was and is in constant flux, which can, of course, be said of art "styles" in general. Early Boston Rockers show a simple rosette in the curved ends of the top slat. Soon a curled leaf, in combination with a modified rosette, puts in an appearance. By approximately 1835, the curling leaf has jagged points and is frequently used without its circular motif, and this is replaced, about 1845, by an elaborate, rather meaningless scroll. This scroll may well be an influence of the French school of design which was making itself felt in the French revival of those days. We find freehand, realistically painted flowers, as used by French decorators, on some of the best chairs of that period. They were among the first designs in natural colors used on American chairs since the Adam-Hepplewhite era. Perhaps the general public was tiring of so much stencilling and felt the need of a different type of design.

William Eaton (1819–1904) for a fuller account of whom see Florence Wright's chapter on the Golden Age of Stencilling, liked to combine a painted design with stencils. His motifs included roses, shells, flowers, and fruit, but he used the rose most frequently. Rockers decorated by him fall in the finest period of the Boston rocker. The stencilled rocker *(Fig. 50)* could very well be attributed to him. George Lord, the last of the old chair decorators, to whom Esther Stevens Brazer was indebted for such a splendid start on her research, said of William Eaton, "the best worker of them all."

Unfortunately we do not know the names of most of the fine ornamenters who were called in by furniture makers to decorate chairs, nor of those who were able to construct *and* ornament their furniture. They rarely signed their work and if labels were attached, they have meanwhile been lost. Bills of sale are often all we have to go by. A notable exception is John White of Woodstock, Vermont, about whom Bernice Drury tells explicitly in her chapter on the Windsor chair. That he made and decorated very fine rockers is proved in Fig. 6. Figs. 42, 43 and 44 show some very fine stencilled rockers by Robinson of Rochester.

We find examples of practically all our American chairs among our rocking chairs— Pennsylvania German *(Fig. 56)* slatback *(Fig. 1)* innumerable Windsors, culminating in the Boston Rocker, even the Southern Empire Style chair has been converted into a rocking chair in Fig. 58. The rocker arrived, designed for an unpretentious setting, and it came to stay. In the Victorian era it even found its way into the parlor. But by then wood and cane had been practically abandoned for horsehair upholstery and tassels, fine painting and stencilling had ceded to ornate wood carving and the American standard rocker, sometimes called the platform or spring rocker, had squeaked its way into popularity. The rocking chair is at its best and finest, as are most chair types and art forms, in its earlier stages, before mass demand and production robbed it of its simplicity, lightness, and grace and the delicacy of its ornamentation.

FIG. 1. *Slat-back stencilled rocking chair. Resembles the early Shaker chair.*
Owner unknown. Courtesy of Florence E. Wright.

FIG. 1a. *Close-up of chair in Fig. 1.*

FIG. 2. *A Philadelphia comb-back Windsor chair converted into a rocking chair. Decoration on the top slat barely visible. c. 1760–1770.*
Present owner unknown. Courtesy of J. J. Shay.

FIG. 3. *A remarkable painted Windsor rocking chair. c. 1800. High framed back and bamboo turnings.*
Present owner unknown.

FIG. 4. *A low-back stepped-down Windsor rocking chair. Date 1800–1810. Painted white with pale green painted decoration.*
Courtesy Mrs. Carl Gilbert, Ithaca, New York

FIG. 5. *Low-back Windsor rocking chair. Painted decoration. Date 1800–1810.*
Present owner unknown

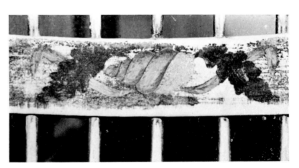

FIG. 6a *Close-up, showing shell in the design on lower slat of chair in Fig. 6.*

FIG. 6. *An original John White comb-back rocking chair.*
Courtesy Mr. N. Grier Parke

FIG. 7. *Delicate comb-back Windsor rocking chair with painted decoration. Dark brown background. White flowers with vermilion accents.*
From the Oldham Collection. Authentic restoration by E. S. Brazer. Similar to Fig. 21, Chapter III.

FIG. 8. *A similar type as Fig. 7. c. 1800–1810.*
Present owner unknown.

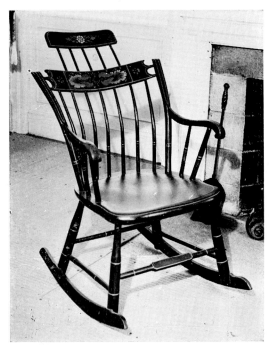

FIG. 9. *Stencilled comb-back Windsor rocking chair. Lacks the delicacy of the John White chairs.*
Courtesy Mr. N. Grier Parke

FIG. 10. *Late comb-back Windsor rocking chair with arrow slats. Painted brown, decorated with freehand designs. c. 1820.*
Owned by Mr. & Mrs. Donald Mason, Granville, New York. Courtesy of Florence E. Wright.

FIG. 11. *Similar type chair, now in Concord Museum, Concord, Massachusetts.*
Courtesy Florence E. Wright.

FIG. 12. *Late comb-back Windsor rocking chair with fine stencilling, arrow spindles, mottled back-ground. Present owner unknown*

FIG. 13. *A late New Hampshire type rocking chair. Only the white tulip in the decoration shows in the photograph. Sprays of green and yellow leaves fail to be recorded. Date 1825–1830. Present owner unknown*

FIG. 14. *An interesting variation in a painted Windsor rocking chair. Coloring is pearl grey with soft green striping and painted ornamentation. Top slat has unfortunately lost its original painting. Present owner unknown*

FIG. 15. Stencilled slat-back Windsor rocking-chair.
The pattern on the top slat matches one in the Cook
collection of stencils, at Saratoga, New York.
Photograph taken by E. S. Brazer. Courtesy of J. J.
Shay.

FIGS. 16 & 16a. Small Windsor rocking chair with Sheraton influence in the back, also in the bamboo turnings. Background is brown. Design painted in shades of green with yellow outlines and accents of yellow and black.
Courtesy of Mr. & Mrs. Nathan Andrews, Westborough, Massachusetts.

FIG. 17. *Two converted chairs. On the left a child's Hitchcock. The ball feet were removed before adding the rockers. Right, a Windsor arrow-back. Note equidistant rockers, rare on so late, converted chairs.*

FIGS. 18 & 18a. *High-back rocking chair, attributed to Lambert Hitchcock. A forerunner of the Boston rocker. The very high back has the pillow top. The narrow slats are connected by three finely shaped arrow spindles. Note that the arms extend below the rush seat, the rockers seem to be equidistant and are short and stubby.*

FIG. 19. *Windsor rocking chair painted yellow, natural wood arms.*
Collection of Mrs. Arthur J. Oldham

FIG. 20. *An interesting yellow Windsor rocking chair, natural wood arms.*
Present owner unknown

FIG. 20a. *Label on top of back slat of chair in Fig. 20. "Joel Pratt. Junior, Sterling, Massachusetts."*

FIG. 21. *An early Boston rocker, signed "Hitchcock and Alford, Hitchcocksville, Conn. Warranted." Date c. 1835. Decoration: stencilling and freehand yellow brush strokes.*
Collection of the late E. S. Brazer.

FIGS. 22 & 22a. *Boston rocker painted yellow. Early type. Stencilling and graceful scrolls on top slat. Natural wood arms. Courtesy Mr. & Mrs. Andrew Weil. Lakemont. New York*

FIG. 23a. *Showing close-up of the gold leaf cornucopias and end scrolls and the fruit and leaves, which are washed over with color and modeled in freehand bronze.*

FIG. 23. *Yellow rocker with natural wood arms. An early design combining gold leaf and freehand bronze. Courtesy of Mrs. Carl F. Gilbert, Ithaca, N. Y.*

FIG. 24. *An interesting Boston rocker. No history known.*
Courtesy of Mrs. Carl Kidner, Oak Park, New York

FIG. 25. *Stencilled small Boston rocker. Owner unknown. This shape top slat indicates chair was made before 1840.*

FIG. 26. *Stencilled Boston rocker, labelled "Union Chair Co. West Winsted, Conn."*
Courtesy Mrs. Harlan Mendenhall, Litchfield, Connecticut

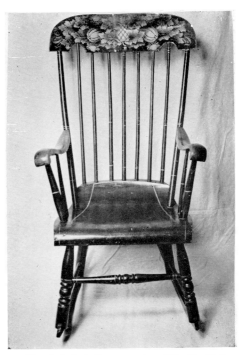

FIG. 27. *Labelled Boston rocker. "T. W. Hodges & Co. Hitchcocksville, Conn. Warranted."*
Owner unknown

FIG. 28. *Small Boston rocker. Higher back than usual. Top slat rolls back. Stencilled basket of fruit and flowers.*
Courtesy of Rowley Historical Society, Rowley, Mass.

FIG. 29. *A small Boston rocker, stencilled with the fruit and scrolls combination typical of the late period. Present owner unknown*

FIG. 30. *The top slat from a Boston rocker showing unusually fine shading in the center, stencilled design.*

FIG. 31. *Late stencilled Boston rocker.
Present owner unknown*

FIG. 32. *Late scenic stencilled Boston rocker.
Heavily grained seat.
Owner unknown*

FIG. 33. *Late stencilled small Boston
rocker. c. 1845.
Courtesy Miss Rose Harrington, Lincolnville, Maine*

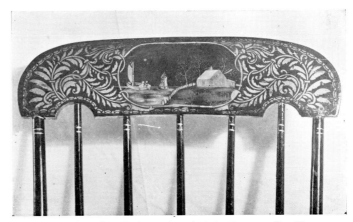

FIG. 33a. *Detail of top slat of chair shown in Fig. 33.*

FIG. 34. *Stencilled Boston rocker with natural wood arms, cane seat. Village scene on top slat. c. 1845. See Cutting and Morrell stencils in Chapter IV, Fig. 56 for design.*
Courtesy Mrs. Walter Dyer

FIG. 35. *Late scenic stencilled small Boston rocker. Front roll has been broken.*
Courtesy of Mrs. Arthur T. Snow, Trumansburg, N. Y.

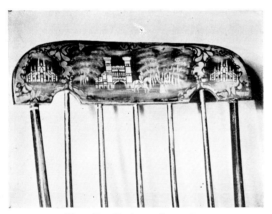

FIG. 35a. *Detail of top slat in Fig. 35.*

FIG. 36. *Stencilled Boston rocker. Design pictures the "Savannah"—first steam-wheeler to cross the Atlantic, 1844.*
Owner: Mrs. Harry Bennet, Fort Edward, N.Y.
Courtesy F. E. Wright.

FIG. 37. *Late Boston rocker. Detail of stencilled top slat.*
Courtesy Mrs. Charles Slaughter, Warwick, New York

FIG. 38a. *Detail of top slat in Fig. 38.*

FIG. 38. *A late Boston rocker, stencilled pattern on top slat commemorates the Wm. Henry Harrison "Log Cabin and Hard Cider" campaign. Called the "Wm. Henry Harrison Rocker," 1841.*
Present owner unknown

FIG. 39a. *Detail of top slat in Fig. 39.*

FIG. 39. *Boston rocker purchased at the "Drake sale," Hampton, N.H. On bottom of chair was written, "H. T. Fay (or Jay) Portsmouth, N.H." Interesting seascape on top slat. Note horizon line!*

FIG. 40. *A late Boston rocker. c. 1845. Elaborate and well preserved landscape stencilled on top slat. Present owner unknown*

FIG. 41. *Boston rocker. 1845 to 1850. Unusual head-piece, with large, crude stencils. Cane seat and sturdy legs nicely turned. Present owner unknown*

FIG. 42. *Late Boston rocker made in the Robinson factory, Rochester, New York. 1850 to 1860. Courtesy Florence E. Wright*

FIG. 43. *Child's rocker from the Robinson chair factory, Rochester, New York. 1850 to 1860. Courtesy Mrs. Fred Guyle, Penn Yan, N. Y.*

FIG. 44. *Another labelled Robinson rocker. Courtesy Florence E. Wright*

FIG. 45. *Late small Boston rocker. Present owner unknown*

FIG. 46. *Small Boston rocker. William Eaton stencil. Collection of Mrs. Arthur J. Oldham*

FIG. 47. *Boston rocker. Present owner unknown*

FIG. 48. *Detail showing front roll on late Boston rocker.*

FIG. 49. *Child's painted and stencilled rocker. Courtesy Mrs. Edward Lloyd, Jr.*

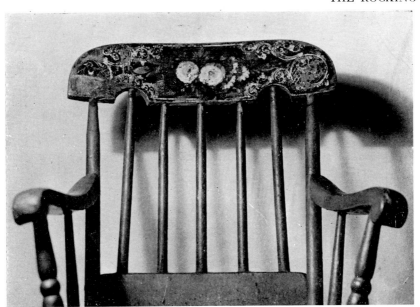

FIG. 50. *Another Victorian child's rocker. Type of ornamentation done by Wm. Eaton. Present owner unknown*

FIG. 51. *Child's rocker with light blue background. Entire design painted. Yellow flowers, green leaves. From Hingham, Mass. Present owner unknown*

FIG. 52. *Yellow rocker. Painted and stencilled ornamentation. Courtesy of Mrs. Vera Brush, Riverhead, N. Y.*

FIG. 53. *Attractively stencilled "Cradle Rocker." c. 1825.*
Courtesy of Rowley Historical Society, Rowley, Massachusetts.

FIG. 54. *A splendid example of a "Cradle Rocker," about 1835–40. The decoration is an interesting combination of stencilling and freehand painting. The stencilling is late type. Note decorative striping.*
Formerly in the Esther Stevens Brazer Collection

FIG. 55. *Crude "Cradle Rocker," with stencilled decoration. Now in Herkimer House, Herkimer County, New York. Courtesy of Florence E. Wright.*

FIG. 56. *Balloon-back rocker from Pennsylvania. c. 1845–1850. Stencilled with colored washes to indicate shading.*

FIG. 57. *Stencilled rocking chair found in Charlottesville, Va. Was in restoration of the room occupied by Edgar Allen Poe at the University of Virginia. c. 1830.*
McIntire School of Fine Arts, Charlottesville, Va.

FIG. 58. *A southern type rocker, stencilled and attractively striped.*
Courtesy Annie A. Folger, Nantucket, Mass.

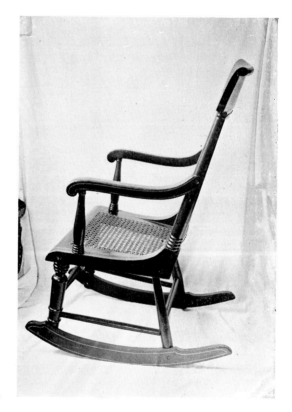

FIG. 58a. *Side view of the chair in Fig. 58.*

NEW-YORK ANNUAL ADVERTISER.

NEW-YORK

FANCY CHAIR

WAREHOUSE.

CHARLES FREDERICKS,

No. 17   BOWERY,

OPPOSITE   PELL STREET,

HAS ON HAND

AN ELEGANT ASSORTMENT OF

FANCY & WINDSOR CHAIRS,

SETTEES & CHILDREN'S CHAIRS

of the newest fashions and well finished, which he offers for sale on
the most reasonable terms.

⁎ *All orders will be thankfully received and punctually attended to.*
Orders from any part of the continent will be attended to with
punctuality and despatch.
A liberal allowance made to shippers, &c.
N. B. Old chairs repaired, painted and re-gilt.

FIG. 59. *From the New York City Directory, 1819.*

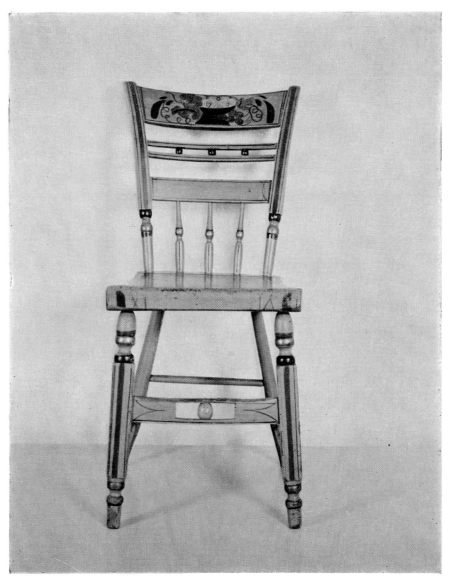

PLATE 6. *Pennsylvania chair. Grey background. Blue-green striping Gaily colored, painted design in red, yellow, and green.*
Courtesy New York State Historical Association, Cooperstown, New York

OTHER TYPES VARY IN SCATTERED LOCALITIES

VIOLA A. BURROWS

T IS BY NOW a well-established fact that English, Scotch-Irish, German, and Swiss settlers found refuge in Pennsylvania in the late 17th and 18th centuries. In the counties in Eastern Pennsylvania, the mingling of the backgrounds of these settlers formed a distinctly hybrid folk-culture. The combination of the English and German languages developed into a speech dialect, neither English or German, which is still spoken.

Bucks, Berks, Montgomery, Lancaster, Lehigh, and Northampton are the counties where we find the descendants of the men and women who emigrated from the German Palatinate, the Lower-Rhine region, Alsace-Lorraine, and the German speaking parts of Switzerland and Moravia. That they and their arts and crafts are so often referred to as "Pennsylvania Dutch," may puzzle those who are not versed in their lore, since Dutch settlers seem to have been as good as absent in their ancestry. Fractura, birth and death certificates, inscriptions on furniture, bride boxes, etc., coming from these regions, are, for the most part, inscribed in German.

The answer, however, is simple. They were referred to originally as Pennsylvania *Deutsch*, but the German word *deutsch* (pronounced *doitsch* and meaning German) was corrupted in pronunciation and spelling to *Dutch*. In referring to them and their type of chair decoration, we will call them "Pennsylvania German," which also happens to be what they prefer.

They were simple folk, these early German settlers, farmers for the most part, who had brought very little with them in the way of worldly goods. They were insular and frugal, their demands were modest, with the result that their furnishings remained crude for years after they had settled in the regions around Philadelphia, referred to often as the Mennonite or Amish country.

The Pennsylvania German chair as a distinctive piece of furniture does not put in an appearance much before 1825, and then it emerges as a definitely robust piece of furniture. We find chairs with so-called "angel-wing" top slats which were typical of the Pennsylvania German chair. The ends of the slat are ornamented with metal leaf, polychrome painting and freehand bronze. *(See Figs. 2, 4 and 8)*.

The balloon-back chair, which gets its name from the rounded shape of its back, was commonly painted a dark brown or green. It was stencilled in bronze powders and washed with bright, transparent colors. A type of the same period was the chair with two straight slats between the uprights. The arrow-shaped splats on Pennsylvania German chairs are heavy and wide, the plank seat is thick; on the Pennsylvania German rocking chair, the rolling front is clumsy. Turnings on all Pennsylvania German chairs are simplified and more bulbous than on other type chairs, the splayed or raked legs are usually heavier. The striping is very wide. In short, the chair is a peasant.

But what a gay peasant! Today the term "Pennsylvania Dutch" has come to mean ornamentation as much as furniture style, although not all their chairs were ornamented. Some of their *best* chairs—they called them their "good chairs"—were made of cherry, birds-eye, and tiger striped maple, and walnut. The Pennsylvania German ornamented chair, however, was colorful. It has been said that the Pennsylvania Germans took decoration into their own hands, and the variety and originality of their work bears this out. On some of their chairs the decoration is entirely painted. Background colors vary from pale salmon pink and pale grey to shades of green, yellow, dark red, and dark brown.

Mr. N. Grier Parke, who sometimes takes time off from the Windsor chair (see Chapter III) and has done research on the Pennsylvania German chair too, writes of a background color used on some called "Dutch Pink," as follows:

"Noah Webster says: 'Dutch Pink. a. The yellow weed. b. A *yellow lake* prepared from fustic or Persian berries with alum and whiting, and used in distemper painting, and for paper staining, etc." Down in Chester County, around Parkesburg, where we had our roots, this was a popular shade a century ago. An old Pennsylvania German decorator named Bittenbender, from whom I first got *the Bug*, told me that this color could not be mixed but must be produced by chemists who know how. We happened on several boxes of the powder some years ago, with which I did over two sets of chairs. Relatives of mine in Chester County have all sorts of furniture in this color, with yellow, umber and dark green decoration—very delicate and lovely work, much more delicate than the general run of Pennsylvania Dutch."

The painted design on the Pennsylvania German chair is not difficult to recognize. It stands out as it is executed in a crude, bold manner and in bright, clear colors. Flowers and fruit were most commonly used, although we also find colorful and primitive scenic motifs. *(Figs. 10 and 11)*. Birds were often incorporated into the design, from the elegant peacock to the common robin and, of course,

their *distelfink* or gold finch. The star was frequently used effectively to complete patterns that were bold, yet pleasing and gay. Always the effect was interesting and distinctive.

The stencilling was not so intricate or unit shaded as its New England counterpart, but it was very effective, due to the wide striping and banding and the shading, which the Pennsylvania Germans handled in their own manner. The stencils were usually cut in one piece and, after being applied, transparent washes of red, green, blue, and yellow oil paint were washed over the gold pattern, giving a "shaded effect." This was a quick and comparatively simple way to give the appearance of hand painting to the chair.

It is quite likely that the Pennsylvania Germans also painted and stencilled their type of design on chairs that were not of home construction at all—slat-backs, Windsors, etc., that had found their way into their region. For we find typically Pennsylvania German ornamentation on non-Pennsylvania German chairs, the slat-back chair in Fig. 12 for example. The Windsor chair in Chap. III, Fig. 23 and the definitely Sheraton influenced chair in Fig. 1 are other examples. But the benches in Figs. 5 and 6 and the balloon-back rocker in Chapter V, Fig. 56 are Pennsylvania German in build and decoration, and a large bright room . . . and large people . . . are really required to accommodate them.

In conclusion it can be said that there seem to be no definite standards to set for the Pennsylvania German chair or its ornamentation. The latter certainly seemed to hinge on the artist's whim and imagination, which have left us a fascinating heritage. The results give the impression of a practical, wholesome people who loved color.

THE SOUTHERN CHAIR

Southern furniture, by which is usually meant the elegant pieces made in Baltimore and Annapolis at the end of the 18th and beginning of the 19th centuries, deserves a book of its own, and there are several. In its day it could be favorably compared to the best that was being imported from England and certainly nothing more beautiful was being made in this country at the time. It was Hepplewhite-Sheraton in influence and developed all the exquisite facets of English furniture: satinwood inlay and veneer, glass inserts, marble tops, and the painted ornamentation ranks with the finest produced in England, with some original features all its own. One of these was the tendency to fine landscape designs on slats. Settees and chairs were constructed to accommodate such decoration.

John and Hugh Findlay were cabinet makers of note in Baltimore. From 1799 to 1815, advertisements in contemporary newspapers attest to their activity there. It is not known whether one of them made the furniture and the other did the decorating, or whether an ornamenter was called in by them, but they produced, among other things, a historic set of thirteen pieces—two settees, one pier table and ten armchairs—on which seventeen different views of Baltimore were painted. Besides scenes such as these, we find bell flowers, acanthus leaves, sunburst medallions and musical instruments painted on Baltimore furniture, altogether much Adam influence in the ornamentation, although the construction remains intrinsically Sheraton influenced.

In Figs. 19 and 20 we have examples of a Sheraton type chair and settee made in Balti-

more, *circa* 1800. Fortunately many pieces of the Baltimore-Sheraton era are well documented and still available for study in museums. (The Baltimore Museum of Art and Winthertur). The settees and chair are marked on the back: *Thos. Renshaw, No. 32 Gay St. Balti—John Barnhart, Ornamentor,* and were once the property of Mrs. Rush Sturges of Providence, R.I. They are now owned by the Baltimore Museum of Art. The back ovals are modified to hexagons and the scenes are local landscapes.

A later Southern chair (1825-1835) known to have been made in Baltimore and Washington, is demonstrated in Figs. 13 to 18. It is referred to as the Lafayette or Washington chair, sometimes erroneously, as the "Southern Hitchcock." It does have a faint resemblance to the Hitchcock chair, however it has its own definite characteristics, one of the most outstanding being the sturdy top slat, which extends beyond the side spindles, and the curved lines at the side of the seat, which are evidence of the Directoire influence. Although its legs are straight and turned (not curved and unturned like the Directoire style chair) still it is often classified as such.

Its place, too, is in an elegant setting. It is an elaborate chair, made of fine wood, sturdy yet well designed, an aristocratic chair.

We find a variety of techniques used in its ornamentation: gold leaf and freehand bronze *(Figs. 13 and 18)* stencilling *(Fig. 15)* and painting *(Fig. 16)*. Ornate designs cover the wide top slat. The striping and bands are gold leaf, when the design is in gold leaf. These are often reminiscent of the earlier brass *ormulu* mounts on Empire furniture. Painted striping is combined with gold bands on other types of decoration, the color of the striping depending on the background color of the chair.

One finds many examples of this chair still used in the Southern states.

THE VICTORIAN CHAIR

"We judge the furniture of Sheraton and Duncan Phyfe by their best examples...we ought not to judge the furniture of the Victorian period by its worst examples," writes Edgar G. Miller in his *American Antique Furniture*. And he is right. The "walnut and horsehair era" as it is sometimes disparagingly called, has given us some fine pieces of furniture and many that were exquisitely ornamented. Tireless effort was expended on intricate design. Gold leaf was used lavishly for framework of patterns—scrolls, arabesques "drips"—work that was beautifully executed and could only be done by expert craftsmen. Flower motifs were popular, many were touched up with pearl shell or nacre. Most of the designs stressed roses, although the fuchsia was used a great deal as well. The leaves were often given form with a precise half-and-half shading of light and dark green. Backgrounds on the late chairs were frequently pastelle. Graining changed from the Sheraton-Hitchcock type to comb or brindle graining. Many caned seats were used on the Victorian chair, occasionally an oval back was caned. Furniture had a distinctly feminine quality, daintiness was nearly always a salient characteristic. The Victorian painted chair was suitable for a lady's bedroom.

We find painted flower groups combined with fine stencilling. William Eaton *(See Chapter IV)* was a master of this type of decoration. But other artists were turning from their easels and applying their skills to the decoration of furniture. The miniature chairs illustrated in this chapter in Fig. 25 were made by the Heywood Wakefield Company in Gardner, Mass. This factory was founded in 1826 and is still manufacturing chairs. The decoration on these chairs is attributed to Thomas Hill. He and his brother, Edward, were employed by the Wakefields. *(Circa 1860)*. They were English and both became well-known landscape painters, the one in New Hampshire, the other in California. They had a method of decorating all their own. Instead of finishing one chair before beginning another, each would group a dozen chairs around him in a circle, dabbing a spot of color on each chair in turn, until finally all twelve designs sprang into being, completed simultaneously. They used black, white, ivory, and grained backgrounds and, for the drips and scrolls, a lovely blue.

These designs remind us of those we find on the Victorian era's sewing machines, typewriters and safes, which were frequently ornamented with fine gold arabesques and tiny roses. The japanners who worked on these probably also ornamented Victorian furniture.

Fig. 28 shows a very fine Boss Tweed chair. One can readily see the tireless effort expended on this fine ornamentation. Gold leaf is used lavishly, the painting is by a master, and pearl shell, or nacre, is used for accent.

When we hear the name "Boss Tweed," we associate it automatically with the corrupt policies of Tammany Hall in the years following the Civil War in New York City. But this is not his only claim to posterity. If William Marcy Tweed had never swindled a cent out of the city of New York and had never been a politician, he would still be remembered today as a fine furniture maker.

Born the son of a chairmaker, on April 3, 1823, he was initiated into the business at the tender age of eleven. The furniture business became too tame for him, so, in his early twenties, he entered politics. As he rose to a place of prominence in New York, his ventures in chairmaking expanded. The chair factory which he inherited from his father was housed in a five-story building at 375 Pearl Street, New York. The business was called *Tweed & Brother* and later the name was changed to *William M. Tweed*. He made the usual line of furniture which included mahogany side chairs of Empire design, others of curly maple with cane seats and many less expensive ones with saddle-shaped wooden seats, reminiscent of the Windsor. He also made different styles of meeting-place benches.

After 1820, the directories designated "chair painting" as a craft and did not list chair painters among the chairmakers plying their trade or operating factories. Furniture stores had their own varnishing, caning, and decorating rooms. Tweed's furniture was sold to the retailer "in the wood," i.e. unvarnished and without caning or upholstery. He sold many chairs and benches to the city of New York at an exhorbitant price and even exported his products to Cairo, Constantinople, Rio de Janeiro, and Lima. Thousands of his Boston rockers were shipped to Turkey.

In 1857, at the age of thirty-four, he forsook chair making in order to devote his full energies to politics. The stories of his making and decorating chairs in jail, after his conviction for graft, are no more than picturesque fables of Americana that grow up around historical figures who catch the public's fancy. Although his politics were corrupt, his chairs and benches were well crafted and are a tribute to his otherwise tarnished career.

With the end of the Victorian era we come to the end of our story of the ornamented chair and its development in America, for the time being at any rate. In this "last act," decoration turns once more to wood carving, furniture becomes massive again, upholstery is in vogue. We see velvet, plush, horsehair, tassels, antimacassars. . . . Any stencilling we may still come across is usually coarse and its execution slipshod. It may be all for the best that we lose sight for a while of painting and stencilling on furniture ornamentation.

Modern furniture, modern homes and ideas have brought their own unique and beautiful designs with them, but many people have remained faithful to the old. For them—for the restoration of their antique furniture and the proper outfitting of the old homes they love, it was essential that the fine, meticulous old techniques be rediscovered and applied. There was a need to step back and explore furniture ornamentation when it was at its best. Esther Stevens Brazer undertook to do just this. The following chapter will explain what she achieved toward this end and what is being done today to restore and reproduce these beautiful old pieces for the homes into which they fit.

FIG. 1. *Pennsylvania chair. Grey background. Blue-green striping. Gaily colored, painted design in red, yellow, and green.*
Courtesy of New York State Historical Association, Cooperstown, N.Y.

FIG. 3. *A "balloon-back" Pennsylvania chair. Stencilled design with transparent wash shading. Usually painted dark green, brown, or dark red.*
Present owner unknown

FIG. 2. *One of a pair of painted Pennsylvania chairs. Stencilled decoration. c. 1825.*
Present owner unknown

FIG. 4. *Pennsylvania bench with attractive stencilled decoration.
Present owner unknown*

FIGS. 5 & 6. *Two interesting Pennsylvania benches. c. 1850. Showing crude type of painted
decoration.*
Owned by Mrs. Harlan Mendenhall

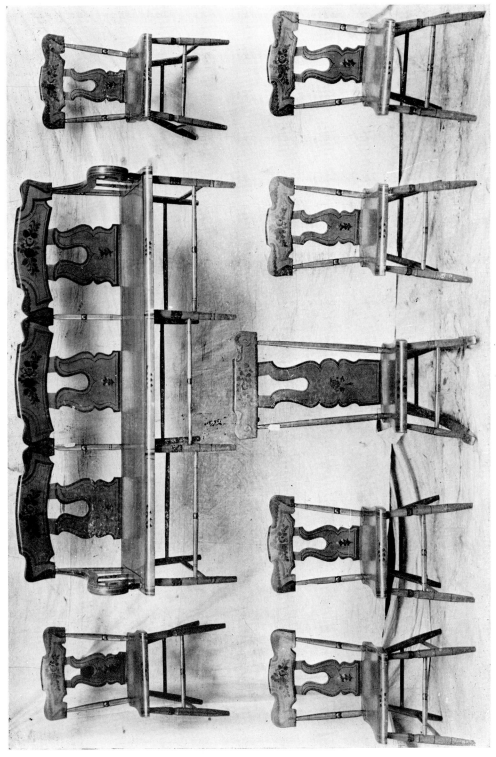

FIG. 7. Set of 14 Pennsylvania (Lancaster) chairs. c. 1850.
Present owner unknown

FIG. 8. *Pennsylvania green painted chair with stencilled and painted decoration. c. 1825.*
Courtesy of Mr. and Mrs. Fred Guyle, Penn Yan, New York

FIG. 9. *Pennsylvania chair. Background salmon pink. Design in green, gold, and black. Freehand bronze accented with brush strokes. c. 1840.*
Present owner unknown

FIGS. 10 & 11. *A pair of Pennsylvania chairs. They have gold leaf trimming, with broad stripes of transparent brown and black framing the scenic panels. The background color is "putty" green.*
Courtesy Shirley Spaulding DeVoe.

FIG. 12. *A Pennsylvania slat-back chair.*
Present owner unknown

FIG. 13. *Black chair, ornamentation in gold leaf.*
c. 1825. Possibly made in Baltimore or Washing-
ton.
Courtesy New Hampshire Historical Society, Con¹
cord, New Hampshire

FIG. 14. *Southern type chair. Background yellow.*
Scrolls, stripes, and turnings are gold leaf. It is called
"the Buchanan Chair," because it was bought from the
White House after Buchanan's administration.
Courtesy of the New Haven Colony Historical Society

FIG. 15. *Southern type chair. Elaborately sten-*
cilled. Black background.
Present owner unknown

FIG. 16. *Pale yellow chair. Design painted in burnt umber and chrome yellow.*
Present owner unknown

FIG. 17. *Southern type chair. Gold leaf decoration.*
Black background.
Courtesy Mrs. Theodore Douglas Robinson, Mohawk. New York

FIG. 18. *Top slat ornamentation is a combination of stencilling and freehand bronze with painted accents. Wide gold leaf band on top slat, with fine black stripe on edge. Gold leaf turnings and leaf motifs on back uprights. Black background, yellow striping. Courtesy Mrs. Carl Larsen, Pittsford, N.Y.*

FIGS. 19 & 20. *Sheraton painted settee and side chair. Sette is marked on back: "Thos. Renshaw No. 37 S. Gay St. Balti (the maker)—John Barnhart Ornamenter." Each landscape painted on top slats is different. Courtesy of the Baltimore Museum of Art*

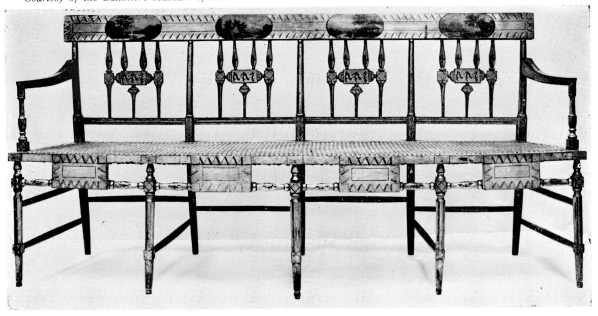

FIG. 21. *Late Victorian chair, ornately decorated with paint brush strokes. c. 1880.*
Courtesy F. E. Wright

FIG. 22. *Victorian chair.*
Present owner unknown

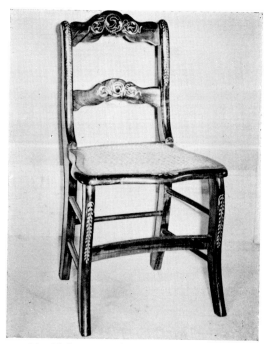

FIG. 23. *Late Victorian chair. Walnut grained. Striped in yellow, with painted rose and buds on top slat.*
Courtesy Florence E. Wright

FIG. 24. *Walnut grained chair with stencilled scrolls, similar to the Cutting & Morrell stencils. The strings of leaves on posts and legs were painted in gold, with freehand brush strokes.*
Courtesy Mr. & Mrs. A. T. Snow, Trumansburg, N.Y.

FIG. 25. *A pair of miniature chairs, made in the Heywood Wakefield Co., Gardner, Mass. and decorated by Mr. Hill. The chairs are black, with pink roses, framed in intricate scrolls. c. 1860. Chair on the left owned by Mrs. Geo. H. Heywood, the one on the right by Mrs. Robert Crouch, both of Gardner, Mass.*

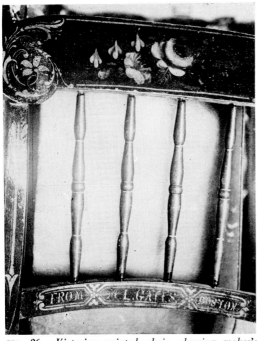

FIG. 26. *Victorian painted chair, showing maker's name on the lower slat. "From M. L. Gates, Boston." c. 1860. Stencilled by William Eaton. Courtesy of Mrs. Chas. M. Auer*

FIG. 27. *Part of a painted bedroom set. Painted by a Boston artist. Background: pale green. Flowers in natural colors. Gold scrolls. Glazed in brown. 1840–1850.*

FIG. 28. *Elaborately decorated Victorian chair attributed by some to "Boss Tweed." Flowers painted in natural colors, scrolls and striping in gold leaf. Pearl shell incorporated in design.*
Present owner unknown

FIG. 28a. *Close-up of Fig. 28.*

FIG. 29. *Same type as Fig. 28.*
Present owner unknown

FIG. 29a. *Close-up of Fig. 29.*

FIG. 30. *A slat-back rocker, lavishly painted in the Victorian manner.*
Courtesy of Mrs. Le Pine Stone, Trumansburg, N. Y.

FIG. 31. *Child's Victorian chair. Wm. Eaton type decoration. Black background with gold scrolls and painted roses.*
Courtesy Miss Hattie Barnes, Ithaca, New York

FIG. 31a. *Detail of Fig. 31. Type of decoration used between 1845 and 1875.*

FIG. 32. *Late Victorian high chair. Simple stencilled scrolls, freehand flowers.*

FIG. 33. *Child's chair with stencilled scroll designs and birds with colored over-tones. Simplified version of the Victorian handwork with its gold leaf and elaborate scrolls.*
Courtesy of Mrs. William J. Schwab, Gainesville, N. Y.

FIG. 34. *Late Stencilled chair.*
Courtesy Mrs. J. J. Storrow, Storrowton, Springfield, Mass.

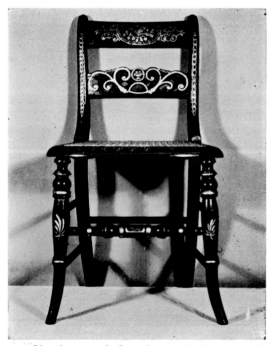

FIG. 35. *Late chairs reflected many of the styles of earlier chairs. Here the Directoire lines with wide stripes are used, and the shaped slats and floral units of the Victorian 1845–1850 style, in simplified form.*

FIG. 36. *An unusual chair, decorated with silver leaf and added color of vermilion, umber, and yellow.*
Courtesy of Mr. & Mrs. Rowe Metcalf, New Milford, Conn.

FIG. 37. *Stencilled chair bought in 1870. The apples and leaves have color used over the stencil. Courtesy of Miss Ruth Howes*

130 ANNUAL ADVERTISER.

HARRISON & SMITH,

HAVE ON HAND

A VERY EXTENSIVE ASSORTMENT OF

CABINET FURNITURE

AND

CHAIRS,

WHICH they offer to the public on as reasonable terms as at any other establishment in this city. They assure their old friends, and those who may favor them with their custom, that no pains will be spared to please those who may call on them, and that the utmost care and attention will be paid to procuring the latest and most approved Patterns.

They solicit a share of public patronage.

REPAIRING DONE AT SHORT NOTICE.

New Haven, June 29, 1841. H. & S.

FIG. 38. *Advertisement which appeared in a Connecticut newspaper on June 29, 1841.*

PLATE 7. *Sheraton chair, restored by Esther Brazer for the Oldham Collection.*

CHAPTER VII

THE INFLUENCE OF ESTHER STEVENS BRAZER ON THE DECORATIVE ARTS

Violet Milnes Scott

N 1921, ESTHER STEVENS Frazer moved into the old John Hicks House in Cambridge, Mass., and became greatly interested in its restoration. She consulted Homer Eaton Keyes, then Editor of the magazine *Antiques*, to find the methods used by the early craftsmen to decorate their furniture, walls, floors and household accessories. At that time little was known about these techniques and Mr. Keyes guided and urged Mrs. Frazer to do research on early American decoration and promised to publish her findings in his magazine.

Her first article was published in April 1922. She continued to write for *Antiques* and many other publications as long as she lived, covering a wide number of subjects. 1940 saw the first printing of her book *Early American Decoration*, which is considered a classic in its field. Her research and writing stimulated a good deal of interest among those who wished to restore and redecorate antiques which they owned.

After considerable persuasion, she consented, in 1931, to teach a few friends in Chestnut Hill, Mass. Later she taught a small group in Wellesley and in her home at Gray Gardens in Cambridge, Mass.

Esther Frazer was an enthusiastic teacher and eager to share her knowledge with her pupils. She made careful notes, drawings and paintings of the early designs she discovered. She spent hours in libraries, historical societies and museums, studying formulas found in obsolete books describing the various techniques used by early craftsmen. At first she had photographs taken of choice examples of ornamentation, but later she took her own photographs and slides. She was constantly experimenting to discover the methods used by the old-time decorators. In addition she meticulously recorded and classified the origin of the decorations.

After her marriage to Clarence Brazer in 1937, she moved to New York and had large classes in New York, New Jersey, Connecticut and New Hampshire, and continued teaching her old pupils in Massachusetts. Many of her new pupils painted as a hobby, some for financial gain, some for therapeutic reasons and others were interested in the history and sources of her patterns.

In 1945, Mrs. Brazer died, leaving many of her research projects unfinished. Nine of her pupils met with Clarence Brazer in Darien, Conn. in 1946, to discuss how her research might be continued. He recommended that a society be formed to keep up and raise the standards she had established, to publish a magazine on Early American Decoration and to have exhibitions and meetings to educate the public in fine craftsmanship and the history of 18th and 19th century ornamentation. This was carried out at Darien, Conn. on May 27th, 1946, when the Esther Stevens Brazer Guild was founded by eighty of Mrs. Brazer's former students. Soon the Guild was qualified to apply for a Charter to become a Historical Society. This Charter was granted by the New York Regents in March, 1952, and the Esther Stevens Brazer Guild became the Historical Society of Early American Decoration.

Today, approximately six hundred members of the Historical Society of Early American Decoration serve the Society and profit from it in various ways. One of the first major achievements was the sorting, mounting and filing of all Mrs. Brazer's patterns, well over a thousand, which formidable task was directed by the Society's curator, Martha Muller. One of the more recent achievements was the removal from Innerwick, (Mrs. Brazer's home in Flushing, N.Y.) of all her research material and her very fine collection of early ornamented pieces to the Bump Tavern at the Farmers' Museum in Cooperstown, where the New York State Historical Association has given the Society a new home.

Members of the Historical Society of Early American Decoration devote themselves to research and writing, to collecting, restoring, and reproducing old pieces, and to teaching.

In response to many requests from widely scattered areas for names of qualified teachers of Early American Decoration, the Society has instituted a Teacher Certification Program. In order to hold a Guild certificate to teach, an applicant must pass rigid standards for both craftsmanship and teaching methods. These standards had first to be established, and this was done through the study and analysis of hundreds of originals in the various categories of Early American Decoration: so-called "country painting," stencilling, the techniques of freehand bronze and gold leaf, reverse painting and gold leaf on glass, lace-edge painting and the exquisite painting found on Chippendale trays. Certificates are issued separately in all these classes. Thus a teacher may be qualified to teach stencilling only; or she may hold certificates in various classes. Because of this program we now have qualified teachers in various parts of the country.

To become a member of the Historical Society of Early American Decoration, the applicant must submit two decorated pieces and pass the standards required in the categories of country painting and stencilling. Later, as a member, he or she can work toward a Master Craftsman Award by being granted "A" awards in all categories. Judges are picked from qualified members and are given special briefing in their work.

The Society meets twice a year, preferably in a place that has a historical background. There is always an exhibition of choice examples of the early craftsmen's art. This enables members to study antique originals and interests owners, collectors and museums in preserving this important contribution to our American heritage. Members' work is also shown at these exhibitions and they can enjoy lectures and demonstrations of various techniques by today's skilled craftsmen.

Recently a Traveling Exhibition of early decoration was set up, for which purpose members loaned some of their own fine originals. This Traveling Exhibition is sent out to various museums all over the country.

The Society also has its own publication, *The Decorator* which is profusely illustrated with fine examples of early decorating and contains articles of lasting historical interest. It appears twice a year.

The years that have gone by since the Guild was formed and the Historical Society of Early American Decoration founded have seen a great development in all techniques of Early American Decoration. More and more research has been done by members, who have shown an astonishing generosity in sharing their findings with each other. This has made for rapid evolution in the beauty and authenticity of today's restorations, reproductions and teaching methods of the Guild. The following pictures give some idea of work done by members. All four pieces were given "A" awards.

FIG. 1. *Green Sheraton Fancy Chair, decorated in metal leaf and freehand bronze.*
Owner: *Natalie Ramsey, Orwell, Vermont*

FIG. 2. *Stencilled Hitchcock type chair.*
Owner: Margaret Watts, Westwood, New Jersey

FIG. 3. *Boston Rocker. Stencilled on crest back and front of grained seat.*
Owner: Thelma Riga, Wilbraham, Massachusetts

FIG. 4. *Turtle-back Hitchcock chair with stencilled slat and metal leaf trim on hand grip, front of seat and posts.*
Owner: Viola Burrows, Norton, Connecticut

BIBLIOGRAPHY

CHAPTER ONE

ADAMS, WILLIAM BRIDGES, *English Pleasure Carriages*, 1837.

BRACKETT, OLIVER, *Thomas Chippendale*, Houghton Mifflin, Co., Boston 1925.

CANDEE, HELEN CHURCHILL, *Decorative Styles and Periods*, Fred'k Stokes, 1906.

CESCINSKY, HERBERT, *Furniture*, 1911.

CESCINSKY AND HUNTER, *English and American Furniture*, 1929.

CHIPPENDALE, THOMAS, *Furniture Designs of Thomas Chippendale*, Gibbings and Co., London, 1910.
———— *The Gentleman and Cabinet Maker's Directory*, London, 1754.

Connoisseur Period Guides—Early Georgian, Reynal & Co., N.Y. 1959.

Connoisseur Year Book, 1951.

DICKENSON, GEORGE, *Papier-mâché*, Courier Press, London, 1925.

EBERLEIN AND MCCLURE, *Practical Book of Period Furniture*, Garden City Pub. 1927.

EDWARDS, RALPH AND M. JOURDAIN, *Georgian Cabinet Makers.*

EDWARDS, RALPH AND PERCY MACQUOID, *The Dictionary of English Furniture*, Country Life. Ltd. 1924–27.

ELLWOOD, GEORGE MONTAGUE, *English Furniture and Decoration*, 1909.

HEINEMANN, WM., *Angelica Kauffmann*, London, 1954.

HEPPLEWHITE, A. & CO., *The Cabinet Maker and Upholsterer's Guide*, London, 1788.

JOURDAIN, MARGARET, *English Furniture of the 18th Century*, Country Life Ltd., London, 1950.

MACQUOID, PERCY, English Furniture, *The Age of Satinwood.*

REVEIR-HOPKINS, A. E. *Old Furniture-Sheraton*, Wm. Heinemann, 1922.

SHERATON, THOMAS, *Cabinet Maker and Upholsterer's Drawing Book*, London, 1791.

SYMONDS, R. W. *Furniture Making in 17th and 18th Century England.*
———— *Masterpieces of English Furniture & Clocks*, B. T. Botsford, London.

VICTORIA AND ALBERT MUSEUM, *English Chairs.*
———— *Georgian Furniture.*

CHAPTER TWO

ARONSON, JOSEPH, *The Book of Furniture and Decoration*, Crown, N.Y.

BELL, J. MONROE, *Reprint of 3rd edition of "Cabinet-Maker and Upholsterer's Drawing Book" with Appendix and Accompaniment and all engraved plates*, Gibbings & Co., London, England.

BELL, J. MONROE, *Reprint of "Furniture Designs of Chippendale, Hepplewhite and Sheraton,"* Robert M. McBride & Co., 1938.

BENN, R. DAVIS, *"Style in Furniture,"* Longmans, Green & Co., London.

BURGESS, FREDERICK WILLIAM, *Antique Furniture*, G. P. Putnam's Sons, N.Y.

CANDEE, HELEN CHURCHILL, *Decorative Styles and Periods in the Home*, Frederick A. Stokes, Co., 1906.

CESCINSKY, HERBERT & GEORGE LELAND HUNTER, *English and American Furniture*, Dean-Hicks Co., Grand Rapids, Mich.

CLIFFORD, CHANDLER, *Period Furnishings*, Hall Publ. Co., N.Y.

CROWNINSHIELD, BENJAMIN W., *Essex Institute Historical Collections*, Salem 1888. Account of Yacht, *"Cleopatra's Barge"* read before the Essex Institute, Salem, Mass, June 4, 1888 by B. W. Crowninshield.

CROWNINSHIELD, FRANCIS B., *"Cleopatra's Barge,"* Privately printed, Boston 1913.

DREPPARD, CARL W., *Handbook of Antique Chairs*, Doubleday & Co., Inc.

DYER, WALTER A., *Handbook of Furniture Styles*, D. Appleton Century Co.

——— *The Lure of the Antique*, The Century Co., N.Y.

EBERLEIN, H. D. & A. MCCLURE, *Practical Book of Period Furniture*, B. Lippencott Co., Philadelphia, Pa.

Encyclopedia Brittanica.

GOULD, GEORGE GLEN, *Period Furniture Handbook*, Dodd Mead & Co., N.Y.

HEPPLEWHITE, GEORGE, *Cabinet Maker and Upholsterer's Guide*, A. Hepplewhite & Co.

HOLLOWAY, EDWARD STRATTON, *The Practical Book of American Furniture and Decoration*, Halcyon House, Garden City, N.Y.

JOHNSON, AXEL P., *Manual of Furniture Arts and Crafts*, A. P. Johnson and Co., Grand Rapids, Mich.

LOCKWOOD, LUKE VINCENT, *Colonial Furniture in America*, Chas. Scribner's Sons, N.Y.

MCCLINTON, KATHERINE MORRISON, *An Outline of Period Furniture*, G. P. Putnam's Sons, N.Y.

MILLER, EDGAR G. JR., *American Antique Furniture*, M. Barrows & Co., Inc., N.Y.

NUTTING, WALLACE, *Furniture Treasury*, Old America Co., Framingham, Mass.

ORMSBEE, THOMAS H., *Early American Furniture Makers*, Archer House, N.Y.

PEABODY MUSEUM, *Descriptive Catalogue of Commemorative Exhibition at Peabody Museum*, Salem, Mass. July 17th–Sept. 30th, 1916. Publ. by the Peabody Museum.

SALOMONSKY, VERNA COOK, *Masterpieces of Furniture*, Dover Publ. Inc.

SINGLETON, ESTHER, Furniture, *University Press*, Cambridge, Mass.

——— *Furniture of Our Forefathers*, Doubleday, Page & Co., N.Y.

STOKES, J., *Cabinet-Maker and Upholsterer's Companion*, Dean & Mundy, London.

STRANGE, T. A., *English Furniture and Decoration*, McCorquodale & Co., London.

YARMON MORTON, *Early American Antique Furniture*, Fawcett Books, Greenwich, Conn.

CHAPTER THREE

Decorator, The, Vol. 6, No. 1, p. 15, Publ. of the Historical Society of Early American Dec. Inc.,

DREPPARD, CARL, W., *Handbook of Antique Chairs*, Doubleday & Co., Garden City, N.Y.

NUTTING, WALLACE, *Furniture Treasury*, Old America Co., Framingham, Mass.

ORMSBEE, THOMAS H., *Early American Furniture Makers*, Archer House, N.Y.

ROE, F. GORDON, *Windsor Chairs*, Phoenix House, London, 1953.

Winston Universal Ref. Library (Dictionary).

WRIGHT, FLORENCE E., *Three Centuries of Furniture*, Cornell Extension Bulletin, 672.

CHAPTER FOUR

BJERKOE, ETHEL HALL, *Cabinet Makers of America*, Doubleday & Co., Garden City, N.Y.

BRAZER, ESTHER STEVENS, *Early American Decoration*, Pond-Ekberg Co., 1st Ed. 1940, 2nd printing 1947, 3rd printing 1950.

Decorator, The, Articles by members of the Esther Stevens Brazer Guild. Vol. I #2; Vol. VIII #2; Vol. IX #1.

DYER, WALTER A. AND ESTHER S. FRAZER, *The Rocking Chair*, The Century Co., 1928.

DREPPARD, CARL W., *Handbook of Antique Chairs*, Doubleday & Co., Garden City, N.Y.

DURKEE, CORNELIUS E. AND EVELYN BARRETT BRITTEN, *Articles on Ransom Cook* in the Saratogian, 1927–1928; 1959.

SCHILD, JOAN LYNN, *Articles on Charles Robinson Co.* in the Rochester Times-Union, 1947; 1959.

STEPHENSON, JESSIE BANE, *From Old Stencils to Silk Screening*, Charles Scribner's Sons 1953.

WARING, JANET, *Early American Stencils on Walls and Furniture*, Wm. R. Scott, Inc., 1937. Reprinted Century House, 1952.

CHAPTER FIVE

DYER, WALTER A. AND ESTHER STEVENS FRAZER, *The Rocking Chair*, The Century Co., N.Y. and London, 1928.

IVERSON, MARION DAY, *The American Chair, 1630–1890*. Hastings House, N.Y.

MILLER, EDGAR G. JR., *American Antique Furniture*, Vol. 1. The Baltimore Press, Baltimore, Maryland. 1937.

MOORE, MABLE ROBERTS, *Hitchcock Chairs*. Tercentenary Commission of the State of Connecticut. Committee on Historical Publ., Yale University Press, 1933.

NUTTING, WALLACE, *Furniture Treasury*, Old American Co., Framingham, Mass.

ORMSBEE, THOMAS HAMILTON, *The Story of American Furniture*, MacMillan Co., N.Y. 1934.

PARKE, N. GRIER, *John White, Chairmaker and Decorator*, The Decorator, Vol. VI, #1, Journal of the Historical Society of Early American Decoration Inc.

WARING, JANET B., *Early American Stencil Decorations*. A reissue of "Early American Stencils on Walls and Furniture," Century House, Watkins Glen, N.Y.

CHAPTER SIX

Antiquarian, Vol. 6, pp. 19–21.

Baltimore Furniture, Publ. of the Baltimore Museum of Art, 1947.

DREPPARD, CARL W., *Handbook of Antique Chairs*, Doubleday & Co., Garden City, N.Y. 1948.

KEITH'S MAGAZINE, *The Return of Rush Bottom Chairs*. Vol. 41, pp. 250–252.

LICHTEN, FRANCES, *Folk Art of Rural Pennsylvania*, Chas. Scribner's Sons, N.Y.

MILLER, EDGAR, G. JR., *American Antique Furniture*, 1937.

ORMSBEE, THOMAS, *Early American Furniture Makers*, Tudor Publ. Co., N.Y. 1930.

ROBACKER, EARL F., *Pennsylvania Dutch Stuff*, University of Pennsylvania Press, Phila. 1944.

STEWART, ELEANOR PINKERTON, *Baltimore Painted Furniture*, The Maryland Gardener, July 1949.

ABOUT THE AUTHORS

MARTHA MULLER, who wrote the *Foreword* for this book, is a charter member of the Guild and has been its Curator since its organization. She was president of the Guild, 1950–1951 and taught Early American Decoration at "Innerwick," (Mrs. Brazer's home in Flushing, New York), for five years. She was the first editor of *The Decorator*.

SHIRLEY SPAULDING DE VOE (Chapter I, *Our English Heritage*) is a professional artist as well as a craftsman. She was commissioned by the New York State Historical Society to restore the stencilled walls in Bump Tavern, at the Village Crossroads in Cooperstown, New York. She is a contributor to *Antiques, Country Life* (in England) *The Antiques Journal*, and wrote the section on japanning for the *Concise Encyclopedia of American Antiques*. She is a member of the New York State Historical Association. the Litchfield Historical Society, the Kent and Washington Art Associations and is also a charter member of the Esther Stevens Brazer Guild.

EMILIE RICH UNDERHILL (Chapter II, *Our Fancy Chairs Adopt Sheraton Details*) is a charter member of the Guild and one of the seven members to have won the Master Craftsman Award. She has contributed many articles to *The Decorator*, is a member of the Board of Trustees and has taught Early American Decoration in New York and on Long Island for several years. She studied at the Art Students League of New York and was a member of its board for several years.

BERNICE M. DRURY (Chapter III, *Sheraton influences the Windsor Chair*) was a pupil of Esther Stevens Brazer. She is a charter member of the Guild, and was president of the Guild from 1957 to 1959. She is a certified teacher of Early American Decoration, a Trustee of the Miller Art Centre, Springfield, Vermont, a trustee of Fletcher Farms Foundation, Ludlow, Vermont, and a contributor to *The Decorator*.

FLORENCE E. WRIGHT (Chapter IV, *The Empire Period Produces the Golden Age of Stencilling*) is a Columbia University B.A. and M.S. graduate and a retired professor of Home Economics, Cornell University, Ithaca, N.Y. She was an Extension Specialist for 22 years. She has taught at the University of Texas, Minneapolis School of Art, State Teachers College in St. Cloud, Minn. and was supervisor of Public School Art in Ames, Iowa. She was a pupil of Esther Brazer and a charter member of the Guild.

Publication: *How to Stencil Chairs*.

Author of the Cornell Bulletins: *Three Centuries of Furniture, Refinishing Furniture*, and *Be Your Own Upholsterer*.

She has written articles for *The Decorator*. Since 1952 she has been a partner in *The Work Shop*, Arts, Crafts and Hobby Shop in Penn Yan, N.Y.

HELEN WARREN CHIVERS (Chapter V, *The Rocking Chair Brings Comfort to Simple Homes*) is a charter member of the Guild and was its president from 1949 to 1950. She was a pupil of Esther Stevens Brazer and has taught Early American Decoration in Vermont and New Hampshire for many years.

VIOLA A. BURROWS (Chapter VI, *Other Types Vary in Scattered Localities*) is a charter member of the Guild, presently on the Board of Trustees and Judging Committee. She was a pupil of Esther Stevens Brazer and has been a teacher of Early American Decoration for the last twenty years. She is a collector and dealer in antiques.

VIOLET MILNES SCOTT (Chapter VII, *The Influence of Esther Stevens Brazer on the Decorative Arts*) is a charter member of the Guild. She was a pupil of Esther Stevens Brazer and was president of the Guild from 1953 to 1957. She is a teacher of Early American Decoration and was Chairman of the Standards and Judging Committee for several years. She has been a contributor to *The Decorator* and *Art in America*.

INDEX